Emma

IN. CREASE.

RELATIONAL AUTHORITY

AUTHENTIC

LEADERSHIP

CLAY NASH

WITH

JIM BRYSON

Spring Mill Publishing

Sharpsburg, Maryland USA

First Printing: 2015

ISBN: 978-0-9835857-3-2

Cover design by Diane Helman.

Editing, text design and typesetting by Jim Bryson.

Copy editing by Betty Cooper.

Proof reading by Carol Pinson Carman and Farah Halford.

Dedication

I dedicate the words on these pages to Brian Pinson and Robert Logan Nash.

B rian Pinson received his invitation to dinner at God's house on Oct 31, 2014. Brian was my friend, a spiritual son and my son-in-law. He was a co-laborer in ministry alongside my daughter, Dawn. From the first time I met Brian in Leslie, Arkansas, there was a heart connection. He served God, loved my daughter and exalted his King. Brian is greatly missed, and our lives have significantly shifted since his promotion. I dedicate this book to Brian's memory because the words on these pages were lived out with him through awesome and intentional relational covenant.

Brian, you are mighty among Kingdom believers.

R obert Logan Nash, my firstborn grandson, carries the Nash legacy into another generation. At the tender age of five, while ruminating on the death of my dad, Logan displayed the inherited relationship principle in a remarkable way.

Logan seemed sad, so his mom, Denise, asked if he was sad because Grandpa Bob (my dad) had died. No, he assured her. That was not the reason he was sad. Then with a wisdom beyond his years, Logan informed Denise that he was sad because Pappa (that's me) no longer had a dad to talk with. Denise told Logan not to worry, because Grandpa Bob is with Jesus and Pappa talks with Jesus, so Pappa will be fine. Logan suddenly brightened up and told Denise that he had it figured out. "Me and Pappa will just have to talk more!"

Yes, being relational is a strength, and to see that strength flourishing in your five-year-old grandson makes life good.

Endorsements

When New Life City Church came into a clearer understanding of church order and five-fold ministry, one of our first steps was to connect with an apostolic team of like-faith believers. My first question to the apostolic leader was: *"If we connect with you, how much authority will you have over our church?"* His response was refreshing and encouraging. *"We will only have as much authority as you respect and honor our counsel and direction."* That's Relational Authority and was a far cry from what had been taught to us about church government.

Clay Nash has set forth the principles of authority from a relational position rather than from a titled, hierarchy structure. Since God is relational, our pattern should be the same. Apostle Nash has set forth the dynamics of understanding, applying, and being at peace with authority. It is a great book for anyone who doesn't understand biblical relational authority, has been hurt by authority, or is in rebellion to authority.

On a personal note: Clay has been a dear friend for over 20 years. What has kept our friendship strong and intact is something from his own pen: *"Relationship outweighs issues!"*

Dr. Phillip J. Tutor
Senior Pastor
New Life City Church
Stafford, AZ

Before I read Dr. Nash's book, I did not realize that I had some negative attitudes about authority that needed to be corrected. His book has helped me become comfortable with authority. I understand in a new way how authority works and enables leaders to get things done. As I read, I found the principles so foundational that I prayed God would help me incorporate them into my life. I need this. You need this. If you want to accomplish significant feats in your life, Dr. Nash's book will equip and inspire you. Most importantly, he lives what he teaches.

Dr. Harold R. Eberle
Author and President of Worldcast Ministries
Yakima, Washington

*****

I heard a statement a long time ago: *"Rules without relationship lead to rebellion."* The Kingdom of God is based on relationships. We were created for relationship and to exercise delegated authority over the earth through our relationships, both with our Lord and one another. Father, Son and Holy Spirit function in perfect relational authority and Jesus demonstrated for us what that looks like on earth. My friend Clay Nash is one of the most relational men I know that walks in great authority. What Clay shares in this book combines truth from the Word of God and the wisdom he has gained through his personal experience in walking out relational authority. This is a must read for everyone—especially leaders—who desire to understand Kingdom authority and learn how to function within it.

Joe Nicola
Senior Leader of New Covenant Ministries
Author: *Ekklesia—The Government of the Kingdom of Heaven on Earth*

Authority can be a scary word for many church-goers who have sat under abusive leadership. Unfortunately, I speak from personal experience. But when authority is truly relational—when you walk in relational covenant with leaders to whom God has connected you—you'll find safety, freedom and even synergy that strengthens you.

In his book on relational authority, Clay Nash offers sound revelation and practical insights on true authority, how it operates, and the many ways it benefits believers. Clay is a man of authority who is also under authority, and I believe his honor-based approach to this sometimes difficult topic will set your mind free to submit to and exercise Christ-like authority that opens the door for you to walk in greater anointing.

Jennifer LeClaire
Senior Editor, Charisma magazine
Director, Awakening House of Prayer

*****

My friend, Clay Nash, hits the bull's-eye with his book on Relational Authority. All authority is birthed out of our relationships, grows because of our relationships and functions in and through our relationships. This is a truth that I have lived in for many years. Authority, great or small, is based on relationships.

This book should be in every internship and bible college in America.

Ken Malone
Apostle
Forerunner Ministries

Not everyone could write Relational Authority. Certainly, no one could write it like Clay Nash! Bookshelves strain with tomes on leadership, but Relational Authority makes you stop and shout, "That's it!" Clay Nash flashcards authentic experiences from his own life so basic we wonder how we've lived at all without these fundamentals. At the same time, we glean from a rich heritage, his enriching legacy of relational leadership coming to full harvest in thousands of lives in many nations. I have never seen a better example of relational leadership and apostolic authority blended together than I've seen in the life and leadership of Clay Nash. Tens of thousands of kingdom citizens long for what this book describes. You will finish the whole book eagerly, without stopping, then you will return to hear it speak as you would a father, for a fathering leader speaks to you in its pages.

Dr. Don Lynch
Founder, Ministry Matrix and Freedom Ministry
Jacksonville, Florida

*****

The journey to relational authority is truly a road less traveled. There are many detours and dead-ends along the way but Clay Nash has never given up on the principles he shares in this book. I have known Clay for over 25 years and I believe we are closer now than we have ever been. Thank you, Clay, for not giving up on our relationship. I'm blessed to call you a friend who sticks closer than a brother.

Fred Bennett, Pastor Emeritus
Christ the Rock Church
Memphis, TN

*****

Mention the words *relationship* and *authority* in a group setting, and you are certain to hear all sorts of reactions and responses. We were created out of relationship and for relationship, and we were created to live in the tension of having authority and of being under authority. (Remember Jesus and the Roman centurion.) These same two things are often the source of much stumbling, consternation, disappointment and confusion among people—believers and unbelievers alike. Some see relationships as messy, too much trouble and sometimes, just not worth the effort because of the pain of disappointments, betrayals, and brokeness. Similarly, authority is frequently viewed in an equally negative light due to abuse, misuse, independence and excessive self-reliance. Regardless of all the negativity, we desperately need healthy relationships and authority in our lives. Without both we cannot reach the highest purposes of God for our lives.

In Relational Authority, Clay Nash—my friend and apostle, presents solid biblical and practical truths to help us all walk out God's purpose for our lives in the authority that flows through authentic relationships. The words on these pages are not theory; they are the unpacking of his life's journey with the Lord, with his wife and family and with countless others over the years.

For the last five years, I have been blessed to see the reality of what is shared in this book lived out as I have grown in relational covenant with both Clay and Susan. I've personally grown and have reaped the benefit as other relationships in my life have been strengthened, healed, matured and expanded by nurturing relational authority in my own life. My life is much richer and I am fully convinced that where I am today is largely due to God's gift of walking in relational covenant with Clay and Susan Nash.

The principles, truths, stories and golden nuggets of revelation contained within these pages are greatly needed in our day, and will change your life if you will receive and apply these truths in the trenches of your daily life.

Jacquie Tyre, Apostolic Leader
City Gate Atlanta
Kairos Transformation Ministries

*****

Relational Authority is a strong, anointed book and a message for the Body of Christ. Clay has tackled a subject where there is, and has been, much debate...that topic being authority within the Church. He clearly lays out the truth concerning authority and that relationship is the basis for all authority in our lives. Authority is not a hierarchy, but one in which there is growth, discovery, empowerment and purpose. As a personal friend, I can truly say that Clay is a man of God who lives this message. His life of truth and integrity challenges me to come higher and to be a relational leader who imparts to many and empowers them. This book is a message we all need and I am certain it will inspire you as it has greatly inspired me.

Rebecca Greenwood
Cofounder
Christian Harvest International
Strategic Prayer Action Network

Contents

Foreword

I have many great memories of times with the three ladies in my life: Ceci, my wife; my older daughter, Sarah; and Hannah my younger. Spending time with them has always been special to me.

Of the thousands of memorable days I've spent with Ceci, one exciting excursion on a beautiful Saturday in the spring of '77 stands out. We had gone to picturesque White Rock Lake in Dallas, Texas, where we enjoyed a wonderful picnic. Ceci cooked some of her great fried chicken and prepared potato salad for the occasion. After eating, we sat on a blanket not far from the lake—the setting was absolutely perfect—and enjoyed some pleasant conversation. She had brought along her guitar, and we enjoyed singing a few worship songs; the presence of the Holy Spirit was sweet. In this beautiful setting, on this beautiful day, totally mesmerized by this beautiful lady, I asked her to marry me. Finding me irresistible, she said yes.

Of the many memories made with Sarah, her wedding is certainly one of the preeminent. I recall the pride and satisfaction I felt when she and I danced at her reception. Actually, shifting my weight from one foot to the other while holding her hand and shoulder was about as creative as the dancing got. But that didn't matter. The important part was looking into her eyes, telling her how beautiful she was and how proud her mother and I were. I spent a fortune that day. "Thank you, Daddy," was all the return I needed.

In regards to Hannah, I love to recall the camping trip she and I embarked on several years ago. We found a beautiful spot on a stream in Colorado, and spent the weekend enjoying nature and nature's God. As we drove through Rocky Mountain National Park one morning, a park with views that rival anything in the world, we were also listening to beautiful worship songs she and I love. I'll never forget the tears that flowed down Hannah's cheeks at one point as she marveled at God's majesty and reveled in His love. Happy tears. Peaceful tears. "I'm in love with God and He's in love with me" tears.

What was it that made those days so memorable for me? With Ceci, was it a lake, a guitar, a blanket, and good food? Of course not; those were simply adornments that created helpful ambiance. With Sarah, was it the uniqueness and joy of a celebrative wedding atmosphere? Not really. I've been to many weddings that hold no such memories for me. With Hannah, was it the beauty and majesty of the Colorado Rockies? As amazing as they are, and as much as they "garnished" the day, it wasn't the mountains.

It was the company.

Sparkling eyes, smiles, embraces, laughter, happy tears, and hearts I connected with at a deep level—these made the memories special. It was the lady, not the lake; the girl I was dancing with, not the dance; the passenger, not the drive. Whom you're with matters most in life.

It is appropriate that a book on authority and leadership, written from a biblical perspective, also be a book about relationships. As Clay Nash so brilliantly shows us, effective leadership requires authority; for authority to be honored from the heart and be truly life-giving, it must be relational. We will follow the person we trust, trust the person we know, and know the person we've connected with at a heart level.

My wife and daughters honor my leadership and authority, not because of some legalistic theology, but because their hearts feel safe in mine. They know I would die for them, I think of their wellbeing above my own, and lead them from a posture of serving.

Clay Nash is one of the most relational men I know. I suppose that's why his book is filled with such amazing insights and practical wisdom on relational authority. I'm highly confident that if you fully apply the principles of this book, your resulting growth will allow God to entrust you with increased authority. And those connected to you will be more inclined to follow that authority!

Get started!

Dutch Sheets
Dutch Sheets Ministry

I am very loyal. My greatest strength is that I am relational. My greatest weakness is that I am relational. I hold on to relationships like the man whose hand cleaved to the sword. I don't want to turn loose of them. I have had God tell me to let it go. I don't want to, Lord, because I like having relationships.

Clay Nash
Southhaven, Mississippi

Chapter 1

Authority

Authentic authority flows through healthy relationships.

Authority

Bring up the subject of authority among a group of Christians, and their diverse reactions will be telling. Some will grow uneasy, others will glance at their watches, a few will gaze over their shoulders towards the exits, and one or two will perk up and slide to the edge of their seats. This is because authority in the church is cherished by a few, scorned by others, and mistrusted by most.

Yet, authority is powerful. Without it, nothing would ever get done. Authority is the ability to influence things, including people. The first thing God did after he made man was to give them a job. To get that job done, he gave them authority. Notice in Genesis that God brought all the animals to Adam to see what he would name them. Obviously, Adam had the authority to do what God called him to do, but did he have to name *hippopotamus* with so many consonants?

Everything about God is filled with authority. His love is filled with authority. His correction is filled with authority. His grace is filled with authority. Anything God commissions receives a portion of his authority. When God says to do something, the authority to accomplish it is delegated from him.

> *God said to them, "Be fruitful and multiply; fill the earth and subdue it; have dominion over the fish of the sea, over the birds of the air, and over every living thing that moves on the earth."*

Genesis 1:28

By virtue of the fact that God told man to fill the earth and subdue it, we can understand that man was also given the authority to accomplish this great commission. We can see clearly the importance of authority when we realize that a large part of what mankind lost in the fall was his God-given authority. This is why Jesus' great triumph was in regaining authority—the authority originally given to man. Look at what scripture says about Jesus:

> *Then they were all amazed, so that they questioned among themselves, saying, "What is this? What new doctrine is this? For with <u>authority</u> He commands even the unclean spirits, and they obey Him."*

Mark 1:27 (underline added)

> *Then He called His twelve disciples together and gave them power and <u>authority</u> over all demons, and to cure diseases.*

Luke 9:1 (underline added)

One of the last things Jesus spoke on earth to his disciples before ascending to heaven signified the key aspect of his ministry:

And Jesus came and spoke to them, saying, "All <u>authority</u> has been given to Me in heaven and on earth. Go therefore and make disciples of all the nations, baptizing them in the name of the Father and of the Son and of the Holy Spirit, teaching them to observe all things that I have commanded you...

Matthew 28:18-20 (underline added)

Notice the connection between Jesus declaring his authority and the clear mandate to his disciples, *"Go therefore...."* The disciples received authority and they were sent out.

So why do people today—especially Christians, who are redeemed into the image of God—react so negatively to the subject of authority? Could it be that we really don't understand authority? That it has been mishandled, misunderstood, and mistaken throughout the Body of Christ? In my thirty plus years in the Lord's ministry, I have seen the rich fruit of authentic authority, the ravages of lifeless authority, and everything in between. I have also seen how often authority is abused in the hierarchy of church government.

This is tragic—both the abuse and the fear of the very force Jesus gave his bride for good. Wherever I saw authority abused, a clear pattern emerged. Typically, I saw those in leadership distancing themselves from the people in their care. I came to understand that while this separation might ensure that direction is followed unquestionably—familiarity breeds contempt—in the long run, it erodes a leader's effectiveness among his or her people while destroying trust, respect, and credibility. Authority does not need to be aloof to be effective.

Further, I saw people struggling to relate to those carrying authority. I uncovered a myriad of ways that we approach a leader, respect a leader, and function under a leader—sometimes with marked success, other times with dismal failure.

I have learned that authority is best understood through the concept of relationship. The authority to do anything—healing, miracles, leading people, speaking correction, organizing and directing, building organizations, developing innovative ways of doing things—are all realized through the relationships we forge. These relationships can be with the people we serve, the organizations we work for, the culture we live in, or even with God himself.

To be effective—to be life-giving—authority must be relational. Of course, not all relationships are warm and fuzzy, but they must be fair, consistent, direct, open, and caring. Authentic authority flows through healthy relationships.

Throughout our study, we will be looking at authority, relationships, leadership, and the journey to get there. At the end of our trek, it is my hope that we will have a firmer understanding of the task Jesus set before us: to take the gospel into all the world and to make disciples of all nations. We can only do this with a firm grasp of the true nature of Christ's authority that he has restored to all mankind.

Authority Applied

Authority, leadership, and relationship flow together. Effective organizations require all three. But the key is relationship. Without relationship, authority kills. Authentic authority is relational and it starts with our relationship with God.

From Romans we read:

Let every soul be subject to the governing authorities. For there is no authority except from God, and the authorities that exist are appointed by God.

Romans 13:1

We can learn many things from this verse. For starters, it is obvious that authority is universal—it is everywhere. It pervades all aspects of our existence, and we have as much chance of escaping it as we have of eluding the Almighty himself.

I learned this lesson at an early age. The most dreaded words my mother ever uttered were, *"When your father comes home...."* I knew right then and there that authority was being delegated, and that it would end at...well, at my end. So be it.

Truth be told, it wasn't so much that my dad ever did anything terrible; he didn't have to. Dad represented the final authority in our home. When authority is clearly recognized, it doesn't need to force itself on others. I obeyed my dad because he was my dad. He walked like my dad, he talked like my dad, and he carried the authority of my dad. Nothing to argue with there. In fact, it was an honor to be under his authority. It bestowed life; it was the life which raised me. Because of our relationship, I trusted his authority. I knew I could rely on him to keep me out of harm's way. As tough as Dad could be, it was his love for me that I came to cherish.

At 17, a young lady and I got in a bit of trouble. Now, I hope that doesn't shock my readers. I've always felt that I was the perfect example of Jesus' saving ability. If he could reach me, the rest of the human race would be a piece of cake. At any rate, I had committed some sins and for a moment, it appeared that I might be headed towards a hastily arranged nuptial ceremony. Yet we were both way too young for marriage.

Chapter 1   Authority

When I walked in the door that evening to tell Dad the news, I had two thoughts. One was that he might react angrily at my stupidity, and the other was that he might congratulate me on my hearty virility. Neither one seemed too likely, however, because I knew my dad. I was pretty sure he'd understand the larger ramifications of what my folly might cost me and help me out of this mess. And indeed, he did. His response was, *"Well Son, I never figured you'd be getting married so young. But we'll help you get set up in a house, make her feel welcome, and give you some time off."*

A house, a family welcome, continued employment, and time to adjust. I knew Dad could do all that because he had the authority to provide it. I worked for my dad at the time—we had several businesses together—and he had the power to accomplish what was in his heart. Fortunately for me, what was in his heart was to look after his son, his future daughter-in-law, and his new grandchild. My situation wasn't right, but he was willing *and able* to make it right. He could have thrown me out of the house, out of his life, and out of life in general if he wanted to, but he didn't. Instead, he bestowed life, and his life became my light through those dark and turbulent teenage years.

As it turned out, she wasn't pregnant, much to our relief. But given our close brush with adulthood and all the trappings, we decided to go our separate ways, leaving fornication behind while we enjoyed one last embrace with the innocence of our fading youth.

Dad's authority made that innocence possible. You see, he had authority, but he operated in relationship. His love corrected me and restored me, and I accepted him into my life because of the love conveyed to me as his son. Fortunately, my early excursion into fatherhood was a false alarm, but I never forgot the lesson.

Authority Sensed

Authority can be felt instinctively. I have walked into situations full of chaos and seen them come quickly to order without me having to say a word. This is because people carrying true Kingdom authority cause a shift in the spiritual energy by their very presence. Even though Issac Newton told us that the natural world is moving from order to chaos, the opposite is true under God's influence. The redeemed of the Lord are bringing order to the chaos.

Authentic authority doesn't have to take over; it often doesn't have to do a thing. It just is. When authority comes into the room, it permeates everything from the spiritual to the natural. If the governor of Mississippi—a person of great authority— walked into one of our church meetings and sat down on the front row, it would change the atmosphere, even if we did not know who he or she was. There would simply be a sense of awe. We might wonder what this stranger was doing there. But the authority that he or she carried would have an influence—it would be immediately felt and people would respond to it before they even thought about it.

No truer test of this principle exists than in a roomful of sugared-up preschoolers. I have seen the authority of God come through gifted caregivers to bring instant order to one of these incubators of future rock stars. Miracle of miracles! If God can tame a pack of preschoolers, he can overcome anything. Praise Jesus!

Still, not everyone responds positively to authority. People are either drawn to authority or they are repulsed by it, reacting in fear, intimidation, resentment or hostility. When relationships are healthy, they respond to those carrying authentic authority. Richard Branson, founder of Virgin Airlines (among other companies), is an example of a person who has been very successful applying this principle. People love to work for him because he treats them fairly, operates a transparent organization, and engages them in his vision for the future. Further, the public loves to fly his airlines. Why? Because he commands them to? Because he dares them to defy his wishes? No. It is because he offers an outstanding product that responds to their needs and wants. He understands what they are seeking, and he gives it to them. This is the fruit of authentic authority, and people respond to the life-giving nature of this power.

Now, throughout our discussions, we will be focused mostly on authority in the Body of Christ. The ministry of the Lord is my life's work and where my heart dwells. However, the principles found in scripture regarding authority will work for both Christians and non-Christians. Why is this? It is because when God blessed and commissioned man in Genesis, he did just that—he blessed *man*. He did not bless Christians. He did not bless Baptists or Charismatics or Catholics. He did not bless Muslims or Buddhists or Hindus. He did not bless Democrats or Republicans or Libertarians. Although I have it on good authority that he did bless the Southern United States, I can't prove that in scripture. About the only thing I can say with the backing of God's word is that he blessed *man*. And in response to that blessing, man goes forth and accomplishes what God intended.

Certainly, redeemed men and women should operate in closer union with their Creator. They are blessed beyond those who can sometimes sense God but do not relate directly with him. Christians stand before the Father in clear conscience, seeking his will and receiving his blessing in the blood-bought relationship through Jesus Christ. Hence the difference between the Christian and non-Christian, but also, the commonality between all mankind.

To the best of my knowledge, Richard Branson is not a Christian, but he applies kingdom principles and they work for him. Consequently, his authority is astounding. Before starting several airlines, he revolutionized the train industry in England. It was in shambles until he took over. He was driven to succeed and to make those around him successful as well. It worked.

Authentic Authority

Authentic authority must be discerned from false authority. False authority is not from God, neither does it serve God. It comes from the enemy, and in the long run, it seeks to destroy the things of God. John told us to try the spirits. When someone in our midst is prophesying—speaking words purported to be from God—I teach my people to sense the spirit in which the message is given. The spirit is more important than the words. Before we can allow someone's spiritual energy to touch ours, we had better know the well from which they are drawing. If someone stood up and said, *"Come unto me, come unto me, I am the Lord who loves you and gave my son and I want to bless your socks off, bless you silly,"* we could appreciate the nice words, but unless we can recognize the authority that is on them, we are sitting ducks to whatever is coming through the battleground of the middle heaven.

> *Behold, I send you out as sheep in the midst of wolves.*
> *Therefore be wise as serpents and harmless as doves.*
>
> Matthew 10:16

Discernment, however, goes beyond assessing spiritual words. There is a belief in the religious community that if we place our total lives in alignment (the old word was *covering*) with certain ministries, we are going to give up some liberty but receive spiritual protection. Well, that only works as well as the quality of leadership we are submitting to. If the people in authority are insecure, manipulative, or controlling, the authority they operate from can become smothering. Therefore, it is vital that we come to recognize true, life-giving authority in contrast to that which flows from deeply flawed people.

Let me share an example of this. A while back, we had a lady become a shareholder at our church. (Note: Our church calls members shareholders.) Soon after she arrived, she approached me warily and said in a halting voice:

"I have been running a prayer meeting in my home for about 14 years and I want to know how you feel about it if I continue."

I was dumbfounded. After gathering my faculties, I said, *"Why wouldn't I want you to continue? God knows we need prayer."*

It was her next words that broke my heart.

"Well, the last two churches I was a part of said that I had to shut my prayer meeting down or leave."

After I found my voice, I told her in no uncertain terms to please continue her prayer meeting.

Now, I honored her submission to my authority, but as a minister, I would be anything but authentic if I insisted that this woman shut down the very thing that was bringing life to her and those around her. Certainly, prayer meetings can devolve into situations that God never intended. Gossip can come out of prayer meetings, as can spiritual bondage, even witchcraft (in extreme cases). But we serve a God who leads, empowers, and sanctifies. If someone under a healthy ministry starts going astray, the same authentic authority that serves the organization will correct the course and allow the efforts to continue in a life-giving direction.

When authentic authority is in people's lives, it serves to help them, not punish them. Sadly, Christians have seen the negative side of church authority for so long that we naturally assume that all authority must be negative.

Susan, my wife, often reminds me that we are not in ministry to meddle in people's lives. As she puts it, *"We are not going to become the adultery Gestapo."* Sure, I make mistakes, others make mistakes, and all have fallen and come short of the glory of God. The point is that the correction that keeps us all on the straight and narrow has to come from the loving hand of God through those he appoints to carry his authority. Authentic authority is our friend. Anything less is false and deadly.

In the natural, the average citizen's introduction to the police might not be under the most favorable circumstances. I still recall my first speeding ticket and the fine I had to pay. Worse was the guilt I felt over being corrected by a uniformed officer. He was pretty harsh with me, saying that if I kept driving the way I was, I'd soon be dead. In like manner, many teenagers learn to avoid the police because they are seen as party wreckers. *"Can't drink, can't carry on, can't do much of anything with the police around."* But let those same kids grow into middle-age and face the theft of their property, and their opinions of law enforcement will undergo a radical transformation, especially when that same uniform comes bearing their rescued child.

Authority is our friend if we understand how to operate in it. Remember: authentic authority gets things done. It works together with us for our good. It propels us into greater works and richer lives. It is what Jesus came to earth to give us.

Submission and Responsibility

The more we submit to governing authorities, as we read in Romans 13:1, the more authority we receive. How many people want more authority? Most people I know do, once they understand how it works. However, we will never have authority over anything we are not willing to take responsibility for. I can take authority in my children's lives because when the nurse said, *"Congratulations,*

Mr. and Mrs. Nash...," I took responsibility for them. However, I can't take authority over someone else's children—not in the long term—because they are not my responsibility. That belongs to the parents. Of course, if their children were defacing a property of mine, I would take authority long enough to correct their behavior, because my property is my responsibility. The rest would be up to their parents.

Seen another way, anything we apply our authority to incurs an assignment of responsibility. If I begin to exercise authority over a situation—rightly or wrongly—I will acquire a sense of responsibility for that situation, whether I want it or not. I really have little choice. That is how authority works. It is also how some people worry themselves into the grave. They extend their authority over all sorts of situations and then wonder why they cannot get free of the nagging sensation that it's all up to them; that they are responsible for every outcome; that the world's turning relies on their vigilance. When poorly understood, this dynamic can make a person's life miserable. Think about what is worrying you to death, and see if there is some improper responsibility you have accepted. It just might work wonders for your inner peace.

Authority as Servant

While it is easier to think of those in authority as helping us, it can often be a far stretch to see them as servants. Yet that is exactly what we read in Romans 13:

> *For he is God's minister to you for good. But if you do evil, be afraid; for he does not bear the sword in vain; for he is God's minister, an avenger to execute wrath on him who practices evil.*

> Romans 13:4

The key here is in accepting a better translation of the word *minister* in this passage. That word is *servant*. Whoever bears authority in your life is also a *servant* of God sent to help you. That policeman who gave me my first ticket was certainly not apologetic for the service he was providing, but in the long run, he may very well have saved my young, reckless life.

Here is my takeaway from this verse: *Don't fear authority unless you do evil.* Or, as we read in Ecclesiastes:

> *He who digs a pit will fall into it, and whoever breaks through a wall will be bitten by a serpent.*
>
> Ecclesiastes 10:8

Digging a pit and breaking through a wall is symbolic of defying authority and abandoning its protections. We do so at our peril.

While I will stress throughout our discussion that we should not be fearful of authority, we have to recognize that when we do evil, we are sowing bad seed that will result in a harvest. Sins like rebellion, fearfulness, and unforgiveness break the hedge of God's protection around us and give entitlement for the enemy to do evil in our lives. It's like clicking on that rotten link in a spam e-mail that opens up our entire operating system to a hostile virus, infecting our computer and that of those connected to us.

As we have said, authority enables us to get things done. But this applies to the enemy as well. When our actions give him authority, he has the power to get things done in our lives; things that we would rather not have done; things that Jesus came to undo—the great "Control-Z" from Heaven.

One of the greatest ways we can exercise authority is through forgiveness, for it is a major force in healing. When ministers gifted with inner-healing find people who do not respond well to the healing anointing, the first thing they look for in the person is unforgiveness. If we want the authority of God to work for us, we must go and bless our enemies, forgiving them as Jesus taught us.

Authority goes far beyond determining who gives the orders and who accepts the orders. Authority is at the root of God's spiritual flow in our lives. The little foxes really do spoil the vines; they take vital things from us, a little authority at a time.

Revelation and Knowledge

One of the most important things that I ever discovered in my life's spiritual journey was the difference between information and wisdom. From Colossians, we read:

> *that you may be filled with the knowledge of His will in all wisdom and spiritual understanding;*

> Colossians 1:9

When we first learn something, it comes to us as knowledge. It is only later when we move into spiritual understanding that the information moves from knowledge to wisdom. God brought this home to me in a major way one day as I was traveling. I still remember the place on Interstate 55, where God had me pull over and write these words on a yellow tablet. He said:

"The reason knowledge puffs up is because knowledge is stored in the soul. But the challenge of the application of the knowledge keeps a man or woman from becoming puffed up, and the knowledge therefore becomes wisdom."

This changed my life. You see, until and unless we attempt to apply the knowledge given, all we have is a college degree with no practical work experience. Ever known somebody like that? Full of the answers before they ever learned the questions? We are called to live what we have been taught. Only through the challenge of living out the knowledge we have been given can we come into revelation and wisdom on a subject. Receiving knowledge shows that we are teachable. Applying knowledge shows that we are *transformable*. Through the application of knowledge comes wisdom.

When we lead others, we must live what we teach. In fact, it is easy to get caught up in the passion of the moment and begin teaching things that we don't fully understand or have not experienced. That is when God, in his mercy, reaches down into our lives and holds us accountable for every word we speak. Want to learn something? Teach it. Want to improve an area of your life? Instruct others. Want to see how you measure up in the darkest recesses of your life? Hold others accountable. Wisdom requires effort—the work of living by the Word of God until we get it.

The church lacks more than knowledge. Yes, Hosea 4:6 tells us that *my people are destroyed for lack of knowledge*, but knowledge applied is the beginning of wisdom. We need to acquire wisdom. I know many churches where the people are full of knowledge and no application. Without wisdom, they grow fat and sassy. Sorry, but there is no other way to put it. Everything flows inward like the Dead Sea, and nothing flows out. To counter this, we must give people the opportunity to apply what they are learning in their gifting.

- *Think we should feed the poor?* Here is a map to the poorest section of town and budget for 100 meals.

- *Think that we are not spiritual enough on Sunday morning?* How about leading an intercessory prayer meeting an hour before service?

- *Think that relational authority is not understood in the church?* Why not write a book? (Oh, wait…)

Chapter 2

Leadership

A leader is someone who can take you to a place you don't desire to go and cause you to discover you have purpose there.

Leadership—A Balancing Force

Leadership is authority in action. When no one has authority, then no one is in charge. Consequently, nothing gets done. As authority is exercised, leaders emerge, assuming leadership from the front, the rear, or somewhere in the middle of the pack. You can't have authority without leadership, and you can't have leadership without authority. When mankind was given authority in the garden, he became leader of the world and all that was in it. When Jesus gave his seventy disciples authority, they became leaders in the spirit and began assaulting the powers of darkness.

> *And He said to them, "I was watching Satan fall from heaven like lightning."*

> Luke 10:18

As we seek to understand authority, we must become familiar with its application in leadership. Of course, all people are different, and so there are many styles of leadership: some stronger and more effective than others; some more suited to certain circumstances than others. Here are nine common traits to excellence in leadership.

Forerunner

A leader is a person who moves ahead first. Therefore, true leaders are forerunners.

> *Where the forerunner has entered for us, even Jesus, having become High Priest forever according to the order of Melchizedek.*
>
> Hebrews 6:20

A forerunner is actually a Greek nautical term. When a ship got close into the shore, the forerunner would get out of the ship with a weighted rope and swim towards the shore, sounding the depth so the captain would know how close he could come to shore without running aground. Now, this could be pretty hazardous duty, especially at night or when the surf was rough. If the ship got in at midnight in stormy weather, it could be deadly. But the essence of the forerunner's job was to determine suitable depth for the safety of the ship—not unlike our spiritual leadership today, determining how much depth exists to safely move the organization. As such, a forerunner is a balancing force, mediating between the thrashing waves driving the ship towards a hazardous shore and the need to stabilize with an anchor. Forerunners often feel caught between competing drives and must strike out in the direction that best suits the situation, often in opposition to others who see things differently.

Motivator

A leader motivates others for a certain purpose or goal. True leaders can take a group of people to a place they might not desire to go and cause them to discover that they have a purpose there.

For example, if I proclaim to my congregation that we are going to Hawaii and I am buying everybody's ticket, I doubt there'd be a problem filling the plane. But if I announced a field trip to the worst part of town to clean up a crack house—oh, and bring your bullet-proof vest—I might have fewer willing participants.

The key to motivating people in less-than-desirable directions is to help them discover the purpose in being there. The thought of entering a crack neighborhood is initially intimidating, threatening, and even repulsive. But the vision of saving the distraught souls caught in the web of drugs, violence, and death is inspiring to anyone inhabited with God's redeeming nature. A leader blesses the people with the vision they need to move out into new and challenging territory. We tend to overcome our initial reluctance when we see God's plan in a situation and when we trust the people who are leading us.

Attracts People

Leaders direct people to a certain course of action through persuasion, charisma, and example. And while the first two are important, it is the example set by the leader that seals the deal. See, I can be swayed by a powerful appeal; I can be drawn by personal magnetism. But when I encounter a leader willing to inhabit the same trenches that he or she is calling me to occupy, I know I have found someone worth following. I will listen to persuasion, I will notice charisma, but I will *follow* example.

> *"I'd storm hell with a squirt gun if he was leading the charge."*
>
> Anonymous

My dad taught me this years ago, *"Never expect the people working for you, or whom you are leading, to do something you are not willing to do. Because when they know you are willing to do it, it motivates them. If you need them to stay two hours overtime and you are just as willing to be there on the job site with them, they will stay for as long as it takes."*

True leaders motivate people and lead by example.

Direction and Structure

A leader gives directions and structure to others' work and effort. As such, wise leaders do a lot of consulting with the people under them before ever taking action—they have to ask a lot of questions to learn what is truly going on before attempting to reorganize it. Things like:

- *What are you doing?*

- *Why are you doing it?*

- *Who told you to do this?*

- *What are you expecting to achieve?*

These are important lines of inquiry before any course of action is undertaken. Often, the people in an organization will be just as surprised at the questions as the leader will be at the answers. This is because these are questions that rarely get asked in the business of daily activities, but they must be understood in order to effectively move forward under true leadership.

My dad and I ran many corporations at one time. We could not have been successful without striving for streamlined operations. Today, as an ex-businessperson, I often dream whimsically about starting a consulting service that instructs businesses on how to be more efficient and effective. Based on my experience, I can walk through a car dealership or retail store and envision large improvements that a few small adjustments could make.

Naturally sensing inefficiency is one thing, but knowing what to do about it is another. The deciding factor in true leadership is getting others on board with change, especially if that change affects their lives. It is not pleasant to face a group of people with a new plan if these people feel threatened by the plan. A true leader knows how to enlist others, and can show them the benefit to embracing the changes. Alignment of goals between leadership and follower is key to a successful outcome.

Coordinates Ideas

A leader recognizes and coordinates other people's ideas, bringing diverse outlooks together into a fully-functioning critical mass. Everybody sees life from a unique perspective, and each viewpoint has merit—even the unusual ones. *Especially* the unusual ones.

A Tents Situation

Years ago we bought a 3,000 person tent and hauled it to the Navaho Indian reservation for a series of meetings. We had never set up this tent before, but we had two days to get ready with sound equipment, lights, safety signs—everything required for a major camp meeting.

We arrived early on the first morning and tried to get the tent erected. Of course, it wouldn't have been much of a task to Barnum and Bailey, but it was huge to me. First step was to raise the massive center pole—the proverbial long pole in the tent. I had a group of willing volunteers from the Navaho nation, but they knew even less about tents than I did. In an effort to get the pole in the air, a few of them stood on one side of the pole and pulled on ropes attached to the top. Of course, they could not pull too much without pulling it on top of themselves, so another group formed on the other side with ropes to hold the pole back from toppling over on the guys doing the raising. But they began to pull too hard and the pole began to fall back on them.

Did I mention that neither side understood how to raise a tent?

The pole lurched one way and then another, with cries and shouts of direction coming from all sides. This went on in vain for several tense minutes. All I could see was a massive tug of war with the promise of the pole crashing down on the losing group while the rest of the meeting became a memorial service for the dead and injured. Not an auspicious start to an evangelistic outreach, unless God was willing to raise them.

Finally, in the resolve borne of frustration, I hollered for all the Navahos to stop work and gather around me. *"Guys, we have a problem,"* I cried. They looked at me with hurt innocence. *"Brother Nash, what's wrong?"* I said, *"Too many chiefs and not enough brave Indians. From now on, I am the chief. The Indians have to do what I tell them."* Because they were now listening to me instead of each other—one voice rather than many—we had the pole up safely and were well on our way to completing the rest of the tent. It was not easy telling these eager volunteers that they did not know what they were doing. But the pride in their faces at the finished product erased any misgivings I had about taking charge. And the best part was that nobody left there with a tent stake through their skull.

Leads In Life

A leader leads in all facets of life—he lives a life of holiness to the Lord that others may know and follow. Poor leaders think it is acceptable to lead in one area but ignore consecration in other areas of their personal lives. Yet the gold standard of true leadership is personal integrity as well as outward integrity. I am not saying a leader must be excellent at everything; everyone has areas of life stronger than others. But in all areas of life, we must be answerable to inquiry and accountability. A leader's life is an open book, as much as some would like to ignore this fact. We cannot lead without revealing much about ourselves and our lives.

It is natural to follow someone when his or her life lines up with the principles that they espouse. But no one willingly follows a hypocrite. Again, no leader is perfect; that is not the requirement. It is the heart dedicated to the Lord in humility while pressing forward that garners the respect and support of others.

Instructs and Corrects

A leader carries the authority to lead others by instruction and correction. While it was not pleasant to correct those eager Navajo volunteers in my story above, it was necessary in order to get them to receive instruction on how to get the tent up without killing themselves. In the long run, that benefit made it worthwhile.

Leading in correction is never easy, but it is vital. Imagine a ship with a fixed rudder. Without the ability to make course corrections, the ship is vulnerable to any current or wind that comes along. If we as an organization—as a body—are to more accurately follow our Lord, then course corrections must become the norm. A leader's job is to administer these in ways that bring life and fulfillment to all concerned.

Faces Own Faults

A secure leader will give the people under him the chance to make mistakes. Some of the greatest discoveries in life are made while trying to do something and failing at the initial purpose.

People set out to do one thing and often discover something greater in the process—even if it is simply the folly of their ways.

Obviously, leaders don't always make perfect decisions. But a true leader knows how to recover and learn from mistakes—even profit by them. In addition, they have the ability to produce other leaders by allowing their mistakes for the greater good. At this level of leadership propagation, long-range growth begins to occur. True leadership strength comes when we do more than just work for the organization; it is when we allow others to develop as leaders that our greater contribution is made.

Naturally, I want the people under me to miss the pitfalls and mistakes I have made in developing my leadership skills, but I know this is not entirely possible. They will find ways to make new and novel mistakes that I never dreamed of! Such is the process that we are engaged in. My dad taught me this in a very real and memorable way.

The first day that my dad put me over a crew of six men I was 14 years old. We had a crop-dusting business, and I had to be at work at 3:00 a.m. By 4:30 a.m. we had to have our planes in the air to cover the fields. If we waited too late, we missed our opportunity for the day and it cost us money—plus it angered the farmers who were depending on us. It was hard work and I had a great responsibility at 14. Naturally, I was not a normal 14 year-old, but I did not know that at the time.

Being a bustling youth of boundless energy, I was full of ideas for changes that needed to be made in this lagging organization. So by 10:00 that morning, I had fired all six men. It took me about another hour to look around and realize what I'd done; suddenly there was no one to work. Now let me tell you why I did such a foolish thing: *immaturity*.

In desperation, I tried to cover their work, and I even pulled guys off some of our other jobs. Somehow, we managed to get through the day, although I was exhausted and went home wondering where I went wrong. My dad wisely waited until early the next morning as we were getting up, then he said to me, *"Son, sometimes a warm body is better than nothing at all."* I interpreted that as meaning that it would have been better not to fire them until we had better men— *if* we could have found better men.

Wiser now by daylight, I rehired all six men and had to give them a raise to return. Then I began to learn to work *with* them rather than *against* them. I realized that it was hard for a 40 year-old man to take orders from a brash 14 year-old kid. So instead of telling them what I wanted them to do, I would say, *"I talked to Dad this morning and he thinks we ought to do this."* Because they respected Dad, they listened. But kid or not, I learned and we survived. Oh, and the crops even got dusted!

The teams that are committed to developing people into leadership positions will ensure ongoing growth. Any organization that continues to raise up leaders on a consistent basis causes that organization to grow over the long run.

Vulnerability

A leader is vulnerable. We cannot lead without depending on others. The relationship between leader and subordinates is a true symbiotic relationship; each needs the other. Without a vision, the people perish. Yet, without a people, the leader is just out for a walk.

Vulnerability must be understood in context with accountability. While I am accountable to a presbytery of elders, I am also, in a very real sense, accountable to all whom I lead. I face them directly as I face God who holds every leader in severe accountability for the care of souls entrusted to his or her authority.

No one knows me better than my wife and children. This is because they have lived with me; they have seen me at my best and worst. Next to my family, my people know me, for they, too, have seen me in the ebbs and flows of life. They have seen me succeed and they have seen me fail. They have seen when my vision and authority were clear, and they have seen other times when I have floundered, seeking direction from God and reaching out for guidance in the midst of my struggles.

The people around me see my life most accurately because my success is their success; my struggles are their struggles. We are all in this together. The true nature of leadership—indeed, the true element of success—is in joining with a group of people. Leading is bonding; bonding is relational; relational is revealing. If we cannot accept personal exposure, we are not fit to lead. If we think leadership is solitary, it is, but in another sense, it can never be. As leaders lead people, they become one with the people they lead. The head, yes. But what is the head when not attached to the body? It is dead, lifeless, rotting and soon to be forgotten.

Vulnerability is the price we pay to lead.

Chapter 3

Levels of Authority

In the beginning <u>GOD</u>...!

Different Levels of Authority

People, leadership styles, and situations all differ. Authentic authority varies accordingly. Just as there is no single model for leadership—no vanilla flavor for all conditions—so authority flows from a common source and disperses itself among the peaks and valleys of life. Authority reaches those most in need. It responds to those reaching out for leadership ability—people willing to accept it—and it flows to those seeking leadership, adapting itself to the particular circumstances. Authority is not a rigid staff ruling with unbending administration. Rather, it is a life-giving spirit seeking the cracks and eddy pools dry with need and yearning for refreshment.

Authority is God's blessing on mankind—creatures striving under the Creator's mandate to go forth and subdue the earth, to make disciples of all nations, to prepare the world for the coming bridegroom. Authority responds to man as the heart of love beating from God's chest.

First Level—Sovereign Authority

The first level of authority—the highest level of authority in the universe—is God's sovereign authority. Genesis 1:1 gives us four simple words, setting the stage for all that follows:

In the beginning <u>GOD</u>...

From this, we realize that all things begin with God and flow from God. This includes all authority. Indeed, the first thing God did in Genesis after showing up and making man was to bestow authority. Paraphrased, it went something like this: *Wake up man. Ah, good! Now get to work.* It was with the *get to work* bit that man received authority to do all that God commissioned him to accomplish.

Sovereignty and Control

We must strike a balance between God's sovereign authority and his control. The two are not synonymous.

In Western culture, the concept of God's sovereignty leads many to believe that God is in control of everything that occurs on the earth—every event, every action, every decision. From the bird that flies from our hand to the car that wrecks on the highway; from the volcano that erupts in the Pacific to the cancer that appears on someone's skin; from the child conceived in the fertile womb to the elderly crossing this world's threshold to embrace their maker. The problem with this viewpoint is that it easily gives way to the image of an orderly world ticking off events precisely while a multitude of gears click and whirl in place, each one predetermined by a divine watchmaker.

In truth, our existence, as designed by God, incorporates randomness—stuff simply happens. Further, we have a free will; we make choices. And although they are often influenced by God, he does not ordain these choices. In fact, the Bible shows us that he can be surprised at the outcome of people's choices.

> *And they built the high places of Baal which are in the Valley of the Son of Hinnom, to cause their sons and their daughters to pass through the fire to Molech, which I did not command them, <u>nor did it come into My mind</u> that they should do this abomination, to cause Judah to sin.*
>
> Jeremiah 32:35 (underline added)

While this can be surprising to some in the Western church, the fact remains that while God *can* be in control, he chooses not to be.

When my Dad brought me into business with him, he did not set me up on a stool and say *"OK, son. You just do everything I say, precisely as I say it, and if you don't know what to do in every situation, you ask me and I'll tell you exactly what to do."* No, that would have been ludicrous. He wouldn't have gotten anything done, and me…I'd have been a nervous wreck trying to figure out what I could and couldn't do. Further, our business would never have grown beyond my Dad's ability to micromanage it.

When God created man, he gave us a free will. For example, God did not make you pick up this book. Sure, he might have convicted you or given you an unction to read it. He might have encouraged you or prompted you, but he did not take over your mind and make you open to page 1, 2, 3.... That is not how God works.

Many in Western culture want to believe that God is totally in control. When faced with daunting obstacles, life-altering choices, or events spiraling out of control, we desperately want to believe that God has everything under control—that nothing can escape his infinitesimal manipulation. But if we step back for a moment and assess what got us to these tough places, we will realize that God is waiting for us to apply all that he has given us to find a way out. If our baby cries, do we pick it up, or do we say, "*God is in control; my baby will be fine.*" If I need gas for my truck, do I find the cash and get it filled, or do I say, "*God knows my need and will fill that tank.*"

Certainly, there are moments when God will do each, but remember: it is his choice to intervene just as it is our choice to act where we are able. As creatures made in the image of the force that spoke this world into existence, I'd say we have a long way to go before our abilities are expended.

God is sovereign—he has the ability to be in control, but he chooses not to.

In considering authority in the church, I often find people who expect leadership to operate just as they believe God operates—in total control. Some leaders become the Iniquity Gestapo, leading a holiness squad that goes around imposing external standards on people. These same people think that personal holiness is achieved through exercising total control over every aspect of their being. Their logic is that if it works for God, it must work for them. Unfortunately, God does not operate like that, and neither should man.

Yes, some improvement can be achieved with rigid self-discipline, but it is a short-lived benefit. If your hand offends you, deal with it. If a man hurts others wrongly, lock him up. If you can't go on a computer without visiting certain sites, toss your computer. If you can't control your kids, tie them up. (*No, of course not. I'm kidding. OK?*) Yes, short-term is where we have to start sometimes. But eventually, we must operate as God made us, not as robots following a program, but as thinking, feeling, and discerning beings exercising our free will, making choices and growing in maturity as each experience—good or bad—imparts wisdom to our learning hearts.

Let me stress, however, that God can *AND WILL* intervene when necessary; I have seen this more times than I can count. While it would be stupid to cut the air-conditioning off during church services and let God cool our services (our church is in the deep South), I have seen the wind of the Lord come in Jamaica under a brush arbor when it was so hot that the people worshiping him were about to faint. I have seen gas in cars multiplied. I have seen time multiplied. I have seen resources stretched and the faith of God's people honored to the point of supernatural supply, divine direction, and sovereign intervention. But I have never seen God set people up for failure by honoring their foolish presumption when all they lacked was the courage to use the ability he'd already given them.

God is not in the business of controlling us; he is in the business of growing us.

A hundred years ago, people thought that natural disasters were the hand of God. When I was young (and the earth's crust was still cooling), I placed third in the Arkansas State Science Fair for a science exhibit. I took 4 pieces of Plexiglas and glued them together. Then I blew hot air in there and created a tornado inside the Plexiglas. It ran for three days. (The first indication that I'd make a good preacher.) I was demonstrating that hurricanes and tornados could be scientifically understood. This was quite a departure from the prevailing belief that these violent weather patterns were because God was wreaking havoc on the unjust while testing the faithful.

Man was set in place to subdue the earth. And he's still working on it. It wasn't too long ago that we thought certain women could never bear children. There is a teaching in some religious circles that says: *God opens the womb and God closes the womb.* Some people use this to say that birth control is wrong, and that any attempts to enhance the fertility of the womb are against God's purposes. But these same people will say that children are a blessing from God. So which is it? If a scientifically trained doctor can help an infertile couple, where is the hand of God? It is in man's hand—the self-same man who was created by God with a mandate to replenish the earth and the authority to fulfill that mandate.

An old joke illustrates this point well. A flood was coming, so a man retreated to the roof of his house. Being a devout man, he fully expected God to save him. As the waters rose, he saw a log drifting towards him. For a fleeting second, he considered jumping on the log and floating to safety, but he remembering his faith and thought: *No, it might be risky. God will save me.* As the waters continued to rise, a sailor in a boat passed by and offered the man a ride. *"No thanks,"* said the man. *"That boat looks leaky. God will surely save me."* Finally, as the waters approached the top of the roof, a helicopter appeared and lowered down a rope. The man shouted to the pilot, *"That's alright. That thing could crash. God is going to save me."* And with that, the man slipped from the rooftop, was carried away by the current and drowned. Later, up in heaven, the man stood before the Almighty and said, *"Gee God, I thought you were coming to save me."* To which God replied, *"Well, I sent you a log, a boat, and a helicopter. What more did you want?"*

The Will of God

In considering the extent of God's intervention in our everyday lives, we should also realize that the will of God is not nearly as rigid and narrow as many people make it out to be. For example, many Christians believe that there is just one person to whom they can be married. I often hear rejoicing over finding "the right one" or lamentations over having not married "the right one." My answer to both is always the same: there is no "right one." There are many "right ones." The right union for any person is the one blessed by God.

Of course, at face value, this might seem like a contradiction. However, the truth is wider than we realize. God's blessing rests on the union that he approves. And that union will often be the one of our choosing. As redeemed individuals operating with free wills, God harmonizes with our choices. That is his nature. He is not in our lives to dictate an unbending will over us; he is not above us to critique our every move. Instead, he chooses to be here with us, sharing in our lives, and honoring our choices as we honor him.

I don't believe there was just one woman in the entire world that I could have married. Susan and I just happened to grow up in the same small town, and from the age of 9, I couldn't get enough of her. But what if she had been born in Sydney, Australia, and I had been born in New York City. Well, for one thing, I'd sure talk funny. But for another, God would have had to do some sovereign intervention to get us together. Certainly, God is perfectly capable of doing just that. However, in my experience, God's people tend to find their mates from those around them who match a certain personality type. People look for matches who complement their strengths and supplement their weaknesses. If I hadn't married Susan, chances are I would have married someone a lot like her, and some other devastatingly handsome guy would have married her instead of me.

Certainly, there are times in life when God will direct us by his will—and that will can be very narrow. In the garden, Jesus prayed *not as I will, but as You will*, as he faced the greatest trial of his life. However, this was not the norm. While Jesus told his followers that he, as a son, did what he saw the Father doing, he never alluded to a life where every waking decision was dictated by the Father. Wisdom will know the difference between *God, I need a flight to England*, and *God, which flight are you telling me to board?* The latter is more restrictive and much rarer.

Like many Christians, I went through a time when God was training me to know his voice. During that period, he would speak to me and tell me specific things such as what our next vehicle would be. But today, it's not like that. I have acquired the lessons God was teaching me, and I typically buy whatever car fits us the best. Do I make mistakes? Sometimes. But I also learn from those and go on—with God's blessing.

Yes, there is a straight and narrow gate, but it leads to a place of broad and abundant liberty. As we mature, God not only allows us to make decisions, he *requires* us to make them. In the exercise of our gifts and training, we learn. Common sense is a gift. So is intuition. Experience is a great teacher. When we are right, we rejoice. When we are wrong, we accept the lesson of our mistake and we rejoice. Both ways, we grow.

Chapter 4

Authority of Truth

God does not divorce us from reality.

The Hierarchy

If all authority flows from God, where does it flow to? And what does it look like when it gets there? Authority manifests itself in a variety of ways, being established in a hierarchy. We will look at several levels of authority flowing from God's sovereign authority, starting with the authority of truth.

Authority of Truth

The second level of authority is the authority of truth. Truth, in this case, includes kingdom laws and physical laws—everything contributing to the everyday reality of our existence.

We find many kingdom truths from the Bible:

- The Ten Commandments

- Reaping and sowing

- Giving and receiving

- Seed time and harvest

- Love your neighbor.

In addition to kingdom laws, examples of physical laws include Newton's Laws of Motion, Einstein's Law of Relativity, Murphy's Law of Negativity, and Gravity's Law of...well, Gravity.

The authority of truth is comprised of the principles undergirding the everyday reality that we all experience. We need air to breathe and food to eat. If we dive into a lake, we are going to get wet. If we run our car without oil, the internal friction will destroy it. In order to receive, we must give. If we try to run forever without resting, we will fall over. What we give, we receive.

Our authority to judge, to believe and to act must stand up to the scrutiny of the authority of truth. Is something true or not? Is it factual? Is it real? Does it go away when we stop imagining its existence? Or does it remain despite our perception? These standards must be applied to both the natural world and the spiritual, the latter being more reality-based than the natural, as it is the foundation for all that we see.

> *By faith we understand that the worlds were framed*
> *by the word of God, so that the things which are seen*
> *were not made of things which are visible.*

> Hebrews 11:3

Established by God, truth carries its own authority. As such, it must be reckoned with. For example—gravity is a truth. It's hard to argue with a force that is always there. What goes up, must come down, unless of course you manage to escape the confines of planet earth, in which case you better have packed a goodly supply of RC

Cola and Moon Pies, because there aren't many fast-food joints beyond Terra Firma.

Miracles

Miracles supersede the authority of truth; that is why they are called *miracles*. Moses talked to a burning bush. Elijah raised the dead. Jesus walked on water. So did Peter, until he remembered back to his Hebrew school physics and his brain screamed: *This can't be happening!* Then it stopped happening.

Because God is higher than the authority of truth, we see many examples of God showing up in his sovereign authority and superseding what we know as truth. Sometimes this is because we need him to do it. Other times it's because he wants to demonstrate his power. And occasionally, he does it just because he can. (Even God likes to show off sometimes.) Realizing this, however, we need to be wary of those who would tempt God into demonstrating his ability to usurp the authority of truth.

When I was a boy growing up in Arkansas, there were things I learned not to do. You just didn't do them if you wanted to live. One was to back-talk my dad. (Now *THERE* was the authority of truth.) Another was to mess with poisonous snakes. Yet throughout my life, I have known of religious people who think that handling these venomous creatures in a church service is the perfect venue for demonstrating God's sovereign authority over the authority of truth. Fortunately, these people live near funeral homes.

Yes, the authority of truth submits to the sovereignty of God. But to force God's hand is simply foolishness.

Time and Space

Can a person transcend the laws of space and time? Yes, when God's sovereign authority intervenes. In the book of Acts, we read how God took Philip and translated him away after witnessing to a high ranking government official who was seeking enlightenment.

> *Now when they came up out of the water, the Spirit of the Lord caught Philip away, so that the eunuch saw him no more; and he went on his way rejoicing. But Philip was found at Azotus. And passing through, he preached in all the cities till he came to Caesarea.*

Acts 8:39-40

Yes, God can do that. I have experienced it as well.

Back in the 90's, I met a man from Holland while I was in Washington State. He approached me from a crowd and said, *"Man, I love your preaching! Every time you come to Holland, I just love it."*

Now, I have never been to Holland, and I told him so. But he said, *"I have seen you there three times."* I said, *"I have never been there."* But he insisted, *"Yes, you have."* I could tell this discussion was going nowhere. Then he told me what I'd preached. And yes, it was my message—one I had developed. No one else could have preached it because it was my own unique message that God had given me. The man went through all the points of my teaching and then reiterated, *"I saw you in Holland three times."*

Now, I know this guy is not a flake. He said he saw me, and I believe him. So somehow, sometime, I must have been standing on the earth in two places at once. Sound crazy? It gets better (or worse, depending on your point of view).

I was ministering in Jackson, Mississippi, in an African American church, when a woman was totally healed of HIV. I knew she was healed by the Spirit, and later, her healing was verified medically through two independent scientific tests. On this particular Sunday as I ministered, the choir sang throughout the service. At one point, I turned to where the choir had been standing, and suddenly nobody was there. The room had vanished. Instead of wood-paneled walls and bright choir robes, I saw thousands of people standing in an open field in Africa, singing praises to God. Now, I am not talking about a vision. It was as real; I was there. The smell of the grass, the heat of the sun, the sounds of people.... I fully expect to meet an African someday and be told, *"Hey, I saw you once. You ministered to my village. You can't carry a tune in a bucket but man can you preach!"* That is how I'll know he's for real.

Now, I am known for being prophetic and spiritual to the point of being a little strange, but I am also known for being balanced. So I know that God can do these things, but these are not experiences I try to obtain. I do not enter services thinking *God, translate me today.* I would not get very far if I did. Instead, I enter the spirit seeking God, submitting my life to him, and wanting to serve his people. Anything more would be tempting God to override the authority of truth for my own means.

Truth and Sovereignty

When we start talking about God's sovereign authority usurping the authority of truth, we can get into trouble quickly. To see this, let's step back for a moment and analyze what happens when a miracle occurs. It is a two-step process. In essence, God intervenes, taking a person away from the authority of truth and into the authority of his own sovereign power. This is fine—God can do as he wishes. But the problem comes when people start expecting a miracle so much that they do the first part on their own. They step away from the authority of truth without the second part—God moving them in the authority of his sovereign power.

See, when people step out from under the authority of truth expecting intervention, they are really removing themselves from the authority that flows from God. They are stepping away from reality. And while this can be incredible when God is leading them, it can also be an opportunity for deception when God isn't leading them. Isn't this how Satan got man to disobey in the Garden, separating man from truth by challenging the very words of God? *Did God say...?*

Authority flows from God in an established hierarchy for a reason. Where there is authority, there is protection. If we relinquish one level of authority—in this case, truth—it had better be to embrace a higher authority, and that authority must be God's sovereign authority. The enemy knows our weaknesses; he realizes our vulnerabilities. Man's thirst for the things of God easily shifts to a thirst for the supernatural, and soon, to a thirst for anything outside of normal existence. That's when we can get in trouble.

Do you seek the supernatural? Seek God and he will lead you. Do you crave new experiences? Seek God, and he will provide. Do you yearn for life beyond this tired old town and the people you've always known? Fine, but don't slide into the passenger seat of the first slick driver you meet who promises a one-way ticket to the stars.

> *But seek first the kingdom of God and His righteousness, and all these things shall be added to you.*
>
> Matthew 6:33

When I minister in a church and the supernatural manifests, I always judge it based on the fruit that develops in the congregation weeks later. Do marriages get better? Or do spouses leave their mates? Do the children get better? Or do some land in jail? Do the messages from the pulpit carry the anointing of God? Or does the river dry to a muddy ditch? I want to know the long-term results of the manifest presence of God's authority. Do people's lives get better? Or do they assume a death spiral? I judge the fruit, and the fruit tells me what to do or not do next time.

A Touch From God

I was in the prayer room one Sunday before service at our church in Dyersburg, Tennessee. My son was also there with another young man. During intercessory prayer, I fell back under the power of the spirit and heard someone praying in the Spirit. It sounded like a Native American language. As I lay on the floor, it felt like I was underwater. I could see the other people in the room but they were blurry. When we used to have a pool, I loved to walk up to it on a hot day and fall backwards into the cool water, then sink to the bottom and hold my breath as long as I could before resurfacing. That is how I felt that day as I lay under the power of God's Spirit.

The next thing I knew, I was in the Navaho Indian reservation—the same one where we held a service and erected the tent that I spoke of earlier. Only, I was standing in their church, and I actually touched the Navaho minister on his shoulder. When I did this, he turned to see what touched him, saying, *"Someone is here with us today."* He obviously couldn't see me, even though I could see him, but he sensed me.

I called him the next day and told him what happened. He was shocked and excited. He said, *"I felt the touch, I just thought it was an angel or God."* For further confirmation, I described some things in his building, among them a scoop shovel over on the right side of the building by the back. His reply hit me like a rock, *"Oh my God! You were here!"*

Now, as glorious as this experience was, what if I had come to my church the following Sunday and tried to build a ministry around that experience? I could have pumped up my congregation to start pursuing such things, and soon they would have been contacting others who purported to have similar occurrences. Before long, the emphasis of our services would have shifted away from the glory of God and the redemption of his people, and begin to focus on new and weird experiences. Deception would creep in, and the power of God to save, heal, and restore would be supplanted by the power of the enemy to deceive, pervert, and destroy.

Regardless of how spectacular our miraculous experiences are, we cannot take our eyes from the One whose authority is sovereign. If something is overriding the authority of truth in our lives, it had better be the Lord God Almighty. Anything less is trying to manipulate God for our own fleshly purposes.

Our Motives

In the book of Acts (16:16-24), we read of a girl who had the spirit of divination. She followed Paul everywhere he went, crying out, *"These men are the servants of the Most High God, who proclaim to us the way of salvation."* This annoyed Paul greatly, to the point where he cast the spirit out of her. Of course, she lost the power of divination, and that incurred the wrath of the girl's masters who could no longer profit from her.

Now, was Paul a servant of the most high God? Certainly he was. So what was wrong with what the girl was doing? She was proclaiming the truth, right? So what was wrong? The key is understanding her motivation. The spirit of divination is when you speak truth with the wrong motive. In this case, the fact that the girl spoke some truth from the power of the spirit working in her lent credibility to that spirit, allowing it to deceive others on a grander scale.

It does not take much of an imagination to see that seeking any experience from the wrong motive can open the door for a host of problems. Oftentimes, our motives may seem pure. When I see someone having a spiritual experience, I naturally want the same spiritual experience. Why? Well, to be spiritual, just like them, of course. But in my aspiration, what am I opening the door to? Envy, jealousy, pride—deception that I don't need in my life. In truth, I *am* spiritual. I *am* a redeemed man. I *am* loved by God, inhabited by Holy Spirit, and destined for Heaven. That is spiritual enough for anybody. Even me!

Sometimes our motives are more subtle—pure, but not in our best interest. Back when my Dad and I owned a trucking company, we were so broke that we asked God to increase our fuel mileage. And for a season, he did it. Was that wrong? No. But would it be wrong to expect God to do that forever? Yes, it would. If I need better gas mileage, I should eventually get better trucks. If I need a miracle to get me through a rough patch, fine. But if I am expecting God to override the authority of truth to continually carry my business—a business that obviously is not competitive in the marketplace—then I have another thing coming. God does not divorce us from reality.

Monkey Business

Before I got saved, I was a truck driver. I ran 5,500 miles a week and slept about an hour a day. I lived on pharmaceutical speed prescribed to me by a shady doctor, and I commonly experienced hallucinations on the road. Most of the hallucinations didn't bother me; I was used to them. But I always knew when it was time to take a few days' break when I started having one particular hallucination. A monkey would appear from behind the passenger side visor and begin speaking to me in sign language. That was my signal that it was time to park my big rig for a spell.

Later, after I got saved, I still drove a truck for a while, and I had to ask God to increase my ability to stay awake. I was running many thousands of miles a week but no longer taking speed, so keeping alert was quite a challenge. Fortunately, God answered that prayer. For a season, he would simply zap me into alertness. Then I began to hear Holy Spirit saying to me, *"Clay, time for rest. Clay, I'm moving you in a different direction."* As I learned to obey his voice, he actually taught me a better way to stay awake—praying in the Spirit. I found that an hour of prayer was as restful as a nap.

See, God supernaturally enabled me to stay awake in the interim, but in the long run, the authority of truth—the need for rest and prayer—won out. It had to. We base our lives on truth; we live in truth; we can't deny truth. When we get saved, truth inhabits the waste places of our lives. I learned to drive a truck God's way, and then he moved me on from there.

And the monkey? I figure he must have gotten saved too, because I never saw him again. Perhaps we'll meet up in Heaven someday. Hope so. I owe him a big thanks for getting me off the road when I needed it.

Deception, Isolation, and Identity

When we are removed from the authority of truth, we are open to deception. However, nothing can deceive us until we first deceive ourselves. Most deception starts when we try to get an identity out of something that is inappropriate—something not appointed to us by God.

How do we know when we are departing from the authority of truth and entering deception? A few simple tests applied to our thoughts and actions are helpful.

- How does it line up with God's word?

- What would others think if they knew?

- Are our choices or viewpoints helpful?

- Are our attitudes healthy?

- Is this something I'd want to read about in tomorrow's newspapers?

- Would I need to isolate myself in order to feel good about what I was doing or thinking?

See, we all have a conscience which tells us instinctively when we are trending toward trouble. The questions above only serve to bring out what our conscience is saying—echoing that still, small voice that won't be quiet when we desperately wish it would get laryngitis. So, if our mind is made up to defy our sense of right and wrong, and do something anyway, our only choice is to isolate ourselves from all the things that sound just like that annoying voice in our head. Tragically, being isolated from all things godly is exactly where the enemy wants us.

Being in ministry, I get many invitations to speak at conventions and services. While it is gratifying to be in demand, it can also be seductive, feeding my ego and reaping the fruit of pride. Frankly, I don't need that in my life; who does? To counteract any tendencies in this direction, I always challenge my motives, asking the Lord if the reason I want to go to the event is to feel good about myself, to bolster my status, or to earn a much-needed honorarium. Further, I often check with those closest to me. What does Susan think? What do my elders think? What does my dog think? (*Hey—you don't think dogs know the voice of God? Think again! Mine can part the water in his water dish.*) When I'm sure my motives are pure, then I will consider accepting the invitation.

This scrutiny applies to all areas of my life. Why do I buy what I buy? Do what I do? Think what I think? For example, I don't ride my Harley Davidson motorcycle because I get an identity out of it as a bad dude. Sure, a lot of guys do, and that's fine for them. However, I am redeemed of the Lord. My identity comes from a relationship with my Creator. In truth, I ride a Harley because I enjoy it. And besides, I can't afford a Honda. Hey, nobody's perfect. I guess I'll have a Honda when I get to Heaven. (Do they even *allow* Harley riders into Heaven?)

Remember that the serpent, which is a form of Satan, could not have tempted Eve without isolating her. Even though Genesis 3:1-6 is not specific on Adam's whereabouts during Eve's discourse with Satan, it is clear that he didn't have much to say while his wife was being led down the primrose path to perdition by the future Prince of Dustiness. She was, for all intents and purposes, alone. Ironically, it was Adam's lack of meaningful presence that sealed his own fate.

Had Proverbs been around back then, they could have benefited from reading:

A man who isolates himself seeks his own desire;
He rages against all wise judgment.

Proverbs 18:1

After committing their sin, Adam and Eve further isolated themselves and denied their culpability in the crime—the sure sign that something wrong had occurred. Did they feel like broadcasting to the world what they had just done? No. They hid…from themselves, from each other, and from God.

When we are isolated, the enemy has the ability to pervert the truth of God in such a way that we won't receive it. That is the reason everything in God's word has to be balanced with another word. There is safety in a multitude of counselors, and there is safety in a multitude of words. In my life, the first place this applies is in my marriage. Susan and I make no major decisions without being in agreement, both with ourselves and with God.

When the serpent isolated Eve, saying, *"You will not surely die"* (Genesis 3:4), he was handing her a new identity based on a departure from truth. The original language tells us that Eve was actually taunting Adam, saying, *"Look what I know that you don't know."* In her pride, she thought she had something that Adam did not have. Indeed, she was right.

She had a serpent for a mentor.

Envy and the desire for identities beyond our God-given callings and giftings need to be tempered by the authority of truth. Not everyone in Christendom will have the same spiritual abilities, anointing, finances, natural abilities, or even lifestyle. These attributes differ with individuals. Frankly, some of us are even better looking than the rest! But the same God who gives liberally to all people knows what we can and cannot handle. Not everyone is going to be a millionaire; not everyone can handle being a millionaire. Not everyone is going to have the same spiritual experiences; not everyone can handle the supernatural to the same level. Some people thrive on intense spiritual excursions while others would go stark raving mad as walls melt, a host of Swahili's appear, and the glory of God rises to the sky like a shimmering rainbow from the hearts of a people united in song.

We all have our calling from God. And while it is normal—even healthy—to yearn for (and eventually obtain) things that we naturally desire, it is important to understand that some things are clearly beyond our God-given sphere of talents and abilities.

For example, I know several fine lawyers. (Yes—lawyers can get to Heaven. As long as they don't ride Harleys.) I admire how they operate: handling complex issues with ease, moving multi-million dollar business deals with a phone call, obtaining justice with detailed insight, and navigating today's treacherous legal waters. But there is no way I could be one. I realize this clearly. Sure, I look good in a pinstriped suit and wing-tips. (At least, Susan says so.) But I do not have the temperament for the legal profession. I'm thankful for what I have, and I operate where I am called and equipped.

I don't think it is God's will for everyone to spend days in the throne room while God speaks directly to them. God gives us the grace to live the lives to which we are called. While God is not a respecter of persons, he does respect the unique stewardship, the dispensation that He appoints to a person's life. God treats us as individuals, for this is what we are. He will do things for one and not the other. That's life—we must accept it. And no, we can't run to Mom claiming Dad is being unfair. There is no "fair" and "unfair" with God. It just is.

I know of a man named Raymond Lee (Oop) Shrauner, from Andrews, Texas. Despite the best schooling that Texas had to offer, he could not read or write. Still, this did not keep him from becoming a successful businessman. Then one day, after his daughter was born, he cried out to the Lord, *"God, I want to read!"* Well, God answered him, and Oop lived a life dedicated to the Lord. God eventually called him to college at age 54, where he graduated with honors.

Oop went on to live a spiritual life that was rare: a prophetic life of supernatural endowment and response to the Lord, although a bit strange to the average person. One day, the Lord told him to get in his truck, leave West Texas and drive to East Texas. Now, he had an eighth of a tank of gas and no money. Still, he drove all the way there and still had an eighth of a tank when he arrived.

While most of us admire the life Oop and other mystical people live, let's be clear that not everyone is called to live like this, nor is the mystical life higher or more esteemed in God's eyes. Sure, a supernatural life is amazing. It is rare and occasionally spectacular. But it is no more special in God's eyes than any other lifestyle.

The key to pleasing God is in answering our individual call with integrity and walking in our identity based on the authority of truth. When Peter stepped out on the water, he had a call from God. When Oop drove to East Texas on an eighth of a tank, he was called by God. When Harold Eberle spent three years in full-time prayer, he had heard from God. However, when Ms. Annie—my third grade teacher—decided to enter teacher's college and dedicate her life to teaching rural kids from a farming community, she had no less of a call on her life. And I thank God for her, because unlike Oop, I didn't need supernatural intervention to teach me to read. I just needed the hand of God to help me sit still. (And a little help from the Principal.)

Chapter 5

Conscience Authority

Don't expect everyone to follow your lead.

Conscience Authority

The third level in the hierarchy of authority is conscience authority. It is based on a person's conscience, and yet it will always submit itself to the authority of truth.

The human conscience is the internal governor of man, deciding instinctively between life and death. It is made up of two parts: *co* meaning "two," and *science* meaning "knowledge." This relates to the two areas of knowledge within each of us: divine knowledge and natural knowledge. Divine knowledge is spiritual knowledge— insight into the realm of the spirit. Natural knowledge is what we learn from life on earth—practical knowledge, everyday truths, a database of experience. And while some people would separate these two into categories of good and evil, the truth is that God created both types of knowledge to work in harmony through our conscience.

We must obey conscience authority in order to stay at peace with ourselves and God. When a child gets upset because something is unfair, that is the conscience at work. When we bend down to help a wounded puppy, our conscience is leading us to do what instinctively seems right. When we accidentally cheat somebody and go back to make amends, that is our conscience leading us to peace.

Our conscience also tells us how to take care of ourselves. We don't have to pray about whether or not to change the oil in our car, or brush our teeth, or sleep when tired. We know to take care of ourselves. We don't feel right if we don't.

Finally, our conscience is the repository for learned convictions, be they spiritual or natural. When we acquire knowledge in dramatic fashion, a behavior reflex operates through conscience authority, taking control of our actions before we have time to think.

I related reflexive actions to this story. A blacksmith was making horseshoes one day, and a man came by to inspect his work. After making a few critical comments, the man picked up a newly made horseshoe, screamed and dropped it instantly. As the man held his hand in pain, the blacksmith observed wryly, *"Guess it don't take long to look at a horse shoe, eh?"* From that day on, the man never picked up a hot horseshoe again, and that much is good. But he never picked up a cold one either.

When I was a small child, our house had a gas wall heater with a chrome grill that kept us from getting into the fire. Unfortunately, fire is tantalizing to a child, and that grill would get awfully warm after a while. Suffice it to say, I am branded for life, even after the scars have healed. No matter how cold it got in that room, I never got near that thing again!

Now, while our conscience was intended for good, conflict arises when conscience authority gets confused with the authority of truth. This happens when people substitute their personal convictions with the indisputable truth of God. You see, there is one kind of truth that rests on the word of God for all mankind and another that speaks to individuals through their conscience.

When God issued the Ten Commandments, they were not simply for Moses and the Israelites; they were for all mankind. When Jesus taught us to *Love your neighbor as yourself,* it did not apply merely to the neighborhoods of Judah. But on the other hand, when Paul said: *Let not a woman speak in church,* I have to believe he was speaking contextually. I know this from the wealth of other scriptures where women spoke, acted, and led—all to the glory of God. Further, when Paul said in 1 Corinthians 11:14: *Does not even nature itself teach you that if a man has long hair, it is a dishonor to him,* this did not mean every rock musician is going to hell. (Personally, I suspect that Paul was bald and just a little envious, but…that's another story.)

There are many convictions that good, well-meaning Christians live by that seem to keep them on track with God, but they are not intended for every person, everywhere, forever.

I know some women who, based on a conscience conviction, will not cut their hair, use makeup, or wear pants. While the women influenced by my ministry don't generally share these convictions, I have noted piousness among those who do. The Mennonites of Ohio and Pennsylvania follow strict guidelines among men and women, and they are deeply devoted to God. In the case of these women, their peace comes from following conscience authority, and only a fool would try to "liberate" them from it.

Conscience convictions come in all forms. Some people are convicted about not watching R-rated movies, while others avoid movies all together. Some people will not exceed the speed limit, while others are comfortable speeding as the flow of traffic dictates, but if they get a ticket, they accept the fine without grumbling.

If a person's behavior arises from a deep conviction of their conscience, they need to honor the authority of their conscience. As in all things, it is the peace of God that validates a personal conviction.

> *For you shall go out with joy, and be led out with peace;*

Isaiah 55:12

Individuals

Conscience authority is how God directs us in unique ways, both individually and culturally. At the heart of conscience authority is the realization that not every detail we need to know in life will be found in God's word. Instead, what we need will be found in the protocol and principle of God's word. What is the difference? I will not find a scripture on which types of movies to watch; movies weren't around when the Bible was written. However, I will find scriptures on purity, hearing the voice of God, and setting examples for others. On the other hand, if I was considering buying a flaming chariot or an awesome sword, I might be able to find something more prescriptive.

The key to understanding God's provision for his people is that protocol and principle guide us, lead us, and direct us, but they do not control us.

For example, some Christians favor the moderate consumption of alcohol, while others shun all alcoholic beverages. While both groups operate from a conscience conviction before God, their actions are polar opposites. Interestingly, I can show you scriptures that support either viewpoint.

Just as everyone will not be millionaires, neither will everyone be teetotalers. Paul said that *all things are lawful, but all things are not helpful* (1 Corinthians 6:12). Jesus remarked that *John came neither eating bread nor drinking wine, and yet the son of man came eating and drinking* (Luke 7:33-34). Obviously, Jesus and John operated from a different conscience authority, yet both were submitted to the same authority of truth and ultimately, to God's sovereign authority.

As we noted earlier, trouble comes when we take what God is saying to us as individuals and apply it universally. God created human beings with variety; God likes variety. Anyone who thinks differently should walk along a mountainside at the peak of wildflower season and consider the multitude of colors springing from the earth. Or better yet, stand on a San Francisco street corner in Chinatown at the height of tourist season and absorb the many languages, cultures, ethnicities, smells, shapes and sizes of the humans passing by. And while you're at it, try a plate of Dim Sum.

When I am in Britain, I hear phrases in preaching that are acceptable there but offensive in America. The first time I heard a preacher refer to someone as *a pompous ass*, I was shocked. But that phrase is in common usage in Britain, and does not carry the same connotation as in the United States. On the other hand, the American word *booger* is just slang for something not working right, but in Britain, it is a scandalous curse word. Different cultures have different conscience convictions. And if you order a soda over there, remember that they serve it warm. (If that doesn't get you sent to hell, I'm not sure what will.)

When conscience authority is treated as authority of truth, it becomes easy to oppress people that we disagree with, especially when we hold authority in the first place. When the Jesus movement began among hippies of the 1960's, many churches refused to accept the new converts with their long hair, beads, and bedraggled jeans. The appearance of these earnest converts violated the conscience convictions of certain established denominations, and so they were rejected—forcibly thrown out of gatherings—until they finally formed their own churches and left the denominations in the dust.

Trust Your Conscience

It is vital that we learn to hear and trust our conscience.

Many years back, in Memphis—the city near my home—a liquor store was robbed and the man working there was killed. The police did not arrest anyone for the crime until years later. They finally found the perpetrator: a young lady in Ohio who had moved south with her boyfriend, then robbed the store and killed the clerk.

I remember the case strongly for two reasons. One is that the woman's lawyer's last name was Nash—so he had to be outstanding. But the second reason is that the night of the robbery, I had left that same liquor store with a friend of mine just minutes before the killing.

My friend and I had driven to the store. My dad was about five minutes behind us in another vehicle with a group of guys. We had just closed an important business deal and we were going to celebrate. I remember being extremely uncomfortable in the liquor store, but I didn't know why. I almost said to my friend, *"Hey! Let's get out of here."* Instead, we quickly made our purchase and left. Dad arrived 5 minutes behind us, and he couldn't get in the store because the police had already arrived and sealed everything off.

Near as I can figure, we were coming out of the store at the same time the robbers were going in. A mere minute later, and we could have been lying on the floor next to the dead clerk. At the time, I did not realize that God works through our conscience—even in heathen. Today I know that it's part of a conscience conviction.

Violating Conscience Convictions

No one should ever cause another to violate their own conscience authority. If our liberty hurts another out of genuine weakness, then the authority of truth—love—should dictate our actions.

Paul faced this issue over the eating of food offered to idols. While he had no objections to the practice itself, he concluded:

> *Therefore, if food makes my brother stumble, I will never again eat meat, lest I make my brother stumble.*
>
> I Corinthians 8:13

Here, the authority of truth overrode Paul's conscience conviction that eating food offered to idols was permissible. The lesson is that if our personal convictions harm our brother, we need to rethink them in love. Of course, we need balance to know whether to conform to others' convictions or not.

I was in full-time ministry when I got my first Harley, and when I started riding it to services, many religious people approached me saying things like, *"I thought you were saved 'til you got a motorcycle."* To make matters worse, I had a full beard at the time. When I preached in Pentecostal churches, elderly ladies in walkers would shuffle up, pull on my beard and say, *"Son, when you come out from behind that brush pile, God is going to anoint you for real."* Yet my ministry was just fine, and I never felt one ounce of conviction to do anything differently. So I didn't change.

Here is the bottom line: If you have a conviction to shave your head, then shave it. If you have a conviction to grow a beard, then grow it. If you think motorcycles are of the devil, buy a unicycle instead. But please don't expect everyone else to follow your lead. Practice your convictions before God in private, who will reward you openly. And please leave my Harley out of it!

Chapter 6

Sub-Authority

Trust your people.

The Four Sub-Areas of Authority

The next level of authority below authority of truth and conscience authority is actually a combination of four variants of authority. They are:

- Delegated authority

- Functional authority

- Cultural authority

- Covenant authority

I teach these together because they are interrelated. There is no established hierarchy to them. Often, two or more will work together, and they will trade places in preeminence depending on the circumstances. However, all four of these areas will always submit to conscience authority, which always submits to truth, which always submits to God's sovereignty.

Delegated Authority

Most positions of function—assignments to get things done—are established and empowered with delegated authority. By its very nature, delegated authority means that something or someone is in greater authority over that position.

The law enforcement officer who arrests bad guys has authority, and if we are in our right minds, we respect that authority through our obedience. However, that officer is also under authority—the Chief of Police who delegated authority to the officer in the first place.

When a doctor performs an operation, she exercises life or death authority. Therefore, her orders must be strictly followed by all concerned: hospital, nurses, patient, family, and even other doctors. Yet that doctor is also under authority. The same state board that issued a license to practice medicine can also revoke it. At that point, the doctor's orders would be null and void because she no longer has authority.

As an apostle of God, given to the church as a ministry gift, I am also established through delegated authority. The authority I carry is given to me by God, and is backed up by the presbytery of men and women with equal or greater authority than mine. I respect these people and could not function with integrity without their blessing, just as I could not function without the delegated authority from God.

Fathers and mothers derive their authority from delegated authority. The biological authority to reproduce is from God who created human beings. Likewise, the parental authority to raise children in a family is derived from the delegated authority of our legal system. The fact that children can be removed from the custody of the parents with legal intervention indicates that childrearing is based on delegated authority.

Government officials—even those elected—still function through delegated authority. A couple of United States Presidents found out the hard way that Congress has the authority to impeach a president.

Paul understood clearly the flow of delegated authority for the gifts in the church. In Ephesians, we read:

And He Himself gave some to be apostles, some prophets, some evangelists, and some pastors and teachers,

Ephesians 4:11

Paul's list of gifting is significant because it indicates a hierarchy of authority. However, note that when considering God's delegated authority, it is the functions that are delegated, not the titles. Delegated authority is given to accomplish things. Remember: authority gets things done. My authority as an apostle does not rest on the title; I could care less what people call me (as long as it is endearing). However, I do care about being able to function in my gifting around them. This is important because the authority that I delegate through the church enables others to operate in their authority.

Liberty

Delegated authority is liberty; it evokes autonomy, empowering people to act and grow. Delegating authority means that the person receiving the authority has been given the freedom to make decisions. It also means that they might make some mistakes. That is part of the package.

In our church, we appoint people to serve in various positions. Therefore, they have authority to do their job. Within that realm of authority, I expect our people to act and make decisions to the best of their ability. However, I do not revoke their authority when things go awry. Instead, I expect them to correct the situation, grow from the experience, and move on. However, if they do something that grossly violates the church's standards, I will likely intervene.

For example, in children's church, we occasionally get a child who is difficult to manage. (Not my readers' children, of course. Other people's children.) Given the number of children in our care, when one continues to act out, our caregivers might have to set the child aside for a time, or if things get way out of hand, give the child back to the parent. I understand this, and even though I've had a parent or two over the years object to getting pulled out of service to deal with an unruly tot, I stand by our children's ministry workers. So I can expect to occasionally see a child on a chair in a corner as I pass by the Sunday school room. However, if I saw a child hanging from the wall with duct tape over his mouth, I just might have to intervene.

The sign of true delegated authority is the freedom to act. As an apostle, God does not mandate my every decision. Likewise, when a prophet in our organization operates, I do not expect every word given to be approved by me first. When teachers or pastors under my influence exercise their authority, I do not judge every decision they make. Delegated authority grants people liberty to exercise their authority within established guidelines.

The key to successfully delegated authority is that we don't delegate it to organizations, titles, or offices. We delegate to individuals—people with whom we have relationship. Authority flows *from* trust and *toward* need. If a person in my organization needs authority to get her job done, and if I trust her, I grant it.

Receiving authority from God flows the same way. He resists the proud but gives grace to the humble (Proverbs 3:24, James 4:6, 1 Peter 5:5).

The Marine Corps has an interesting take on delegated authority. When a battlefield commander is faced with a dilemma, he has one imperative: make a decision and move. The repercussions of not making a decision are far greater than making a wrong decision. The Marine Corps understands that under fire, survival depends on decisiveness.

Decisiveness comes from true delegated authority. There is no other way.

Functional Authority

Functional authority arises from a skill set. When flowing correctly, the person best equipped to do the job, gets the job, and carries the authority to get it done.

In our church during Sunday services, we use a sound system run by an excellent sound person. Now, I have often been accused of being deaf in one ear and unable to hear out of the other. (Mostly by Susan, though I suspect it's when I'm not paying attention.) So it would be ludicrous for me to go back to the soundboard, assert my authority, and start tuning knobs. Why would I do that if I have a perfectly good sound person working the board?

Unfortunately, the church has become staunchly hierarchal and has made authority into a pecking order. Yet the true role of higher authority in a church is to carry the greatest responsibility. Functional authority recognizes that there are people far more gifted than I am. Therefore, it is my responsibility to ensure that nothing interferes with their ability to exercise that authority.

The people who head up our worship team are outstanding. They are good at what they do, and they carry the authority to do it. Because of the functional authority on them, I submit myself to them. Of course, that doesn't mean I won't make a suggestion, but ultimately, they have the authority to say, *"No, it's not the right timing; we don't think it's right; it's not gonna fly; you're crazy—this can't work."* I am OK with this level of frankness. In fact, I depend on it.

Our intercession ministry leaders have the same functional authority as any other ministry in our church. I might tell our head intercessor to lead the intercessory prayer team on a 40-day water fast. However, he could be aware of people on the team with diabetic problems, and others for whom such a directive simply would not work in their lives. So he would have a conscience objection that this was not right, and that my motivation could possibly be wrong. It would violate his conscience, and he would be within his authority to make the final decision on the fast.

Those in authority over a church are called to take responsibility for it, not to rule over every aspect of it. Of course, I can hear the other side of the argument: *How can I take responsibility for something that I cannot control?* The answer is simple: You delegate to those with functional authority—those better equipped to handle certain areas. Recall our discussion in Chapter 3 on God's sovereignty and control. God does not control every aspect of our existence, and neither should we try to control everything under our purview.

How do you take responsibility for things you cannot control? You trust your people.

Marriage and Functional Authority

A good place to understand functional authority is in marriage. First of all, we must accept that when God set the husband over the wife, it did not establish rank. The wife is no more a second-class citizen than the husband is a first-class citizen. Both are equal before God. The oversight of husband to wife is based largely on his duties to provide, protect, and serve. Consequently, when one person in the marriage is better at something than the other, authority should be allowed to naturally shift to the person most gifted and able to function in that area.

For example, while the kitchen traditionally has been the wife's purview, some husbands value their ability to cook more than anything they might do in the garage. A friend of mine actually gets irate when his wife uses the kitchen because she moves his spice jars around and he can't find things when flying through recipes, preparing for a dinner party. He commonly shops for food, plans meals, and…yes ladies, he actually cleans up afterwards.

Similarly, if I have a breakdown on the road and have no mechanical ability to fix the problem, but my wife does, she could say, *"Clay, get me a 16 mm box-end wrench, a Phillips-head screw driver, and a can of WD-40,"* and I would jump to it. She has the functional authority here. And hey, if it gets us running again, I'll even let her drive!

Cultural Authority

The next arena of authority is cultural authority. Few people realize that culture carries an authority. This is because it often blends with other areas of authority. The example I used earlier of preachers in Britain using the term *pompous ass* is as much about cultural authority as conscious authority. The English have a conscious conviction that the term is perfectly acceptable because it is ingrained in their culture.

Another example of cultural authority comes from Western missionaries arriving on a foreign shore, establishing contact with the indigenous people, and enforcing behaviors from their own culture as God's mandate. A classic and complex struggle is in the area of polygamy, a prevalent practice in more primitive cultures of the world. When missionaries convince the newly converted husbands that having multiple wives is wrong in God's sight, the husbands often divorce the remaining wives. Unfortunately, the discarded wives have nowhere to go and no means of supporting themselves or their children. They face bleak prospects for survival in those cultures.

Here is an example of cultural authority from the Bible. Jacob worked a deal with Laban to marry his daughter Rachel; he had to work seven years to marry her. However, when the time came, Laban informed Jacob that their culture required that the oldest daughter be married first, so Jacob had to marry Leah and then work seven more years to marry Rachel. While Laban was a treacherous schemer, he was supported by cultural authority, and Jacob had to obey.

As we said at the beginning of this section, all four levels of authority—delegated, functional, cultural, and covenant—are equal, although one can take preeminence over the others. In the story of Jacob, even though Jacob and Laban had an agreement—a covenant— this is an example where cultural authority rose above covenant authority.

Here in the South of the United States where I often minister, we have a wide difference of cultures in churches. Whenever possible, I honor the local cultural authority. Some churches are comfortable with casual dress, so I know I can preach in jeans, cowboy boots, and an open collared shirt. Other churches, however, expect ministers to be in a three-piece suit. Still others—the most conservative—can become offended if my tie is not somber enough. In all these cases, I submit to the cultural authority reflected in those meeting places. Certainly, God can move in a congregation whether I am wearing a three-piece suit, jeans and boots, or a bathing suit, as long as I am not offending the people he is trying to reach. (Yes, people do preach on the beach in bathing suits. L.A.—gotta love it.)

Yet, cultural authority extends beyond our attire. While it is common in most evangelical churches to offer an opportunity to accept Jesus as savior, not all churches follow the same pattern. This difference is a reflection of the cultural authority prevalent in the house. I am familiar with churches who lead converts in prayer (commonly called "the sinner's prayer"). However, other churches will take those seeking God to the front of the church and have the rest of the congregation stand up and cry, *"Welcome to the family of God!"*

The first time I saw this, my religious brain started screaming: *No prayer? No confession? No weeping for hours at the altar while the organ plays "Just As I Am?" How can they be saved???*

Well, the truth is that they are being welcomed into the family of God according to their cultural authority. And if God respects it (which he does—I know many fine Christians who came to salvation in a variety of ways) then who are we to disrespect it?

Paul said that he became all things to all people so he may win the few (1 Corinthians 9:19-23). I know a woman who ministers extensively in Africa. She must always wear a dress when addressing a congregation because it is offensive for a woman's backside not to be covered. So if she did not come under that cultural level of authority, she would lose all effectiveness.

Of course, cultural authority should only be in force when it aligns with conscience authority, the authority of truth, and God's sovereign authority. When Jesus healed people on the Sabbath, he offended the cultural authority of the Jewish religious establishment. However, he did not stop healing. This is because he was under a higher authority—his ministerial calling. Nothing in God's word prohibits healing on the Sabbath.

Following Jesus' example, if I am in a foreign country and they ask me to do something according to their culture, I will first make sure that it lines up with my conscience, the authority of truth, and God's sovereign authority. I will not violate these, even at the risk of offending my hosts.

Now, there have been times when I wished I could have overridden cultural authority. In Africa, it is vital that you eat and drink whatever they put in front of you. To refuse a dish is horribly offensive in their culture. Sometimes this works out well. I have been to places where the local people fed us wonderfully. But I have also been places where it was a bit challenging. In parts of Africa and South America, they have a special beverage called spit beer. It is made by toothless old women who chew fruit and gum it until it is mushy, then spit it into a jar, add sugar, seal it and put it in the sun until it ferments. It is a high honor to be offered spit beer. I could only swallow that stuff by the grace of God!

In Peru, we used to get in a putt-putt boat and take a three-day journey upriver to minister. When we arrived, the locals greeted us with spit beer! Oh, my favorite. We had to drink it; there was no other choice. Then one day—glory to God!—I learned that if you came off the boat with a drink in hand and offered it to the locals before they offered you a drink, they had to drink your drink instead. Amazing grace, how sweet the sound! From then on, we travelled well supplied with Coca-Cola.

Another local delicacy in some countries is turtle eggs. They are harvested from the beach sand and left out in the sun to be poached. Of all that I have eaten in the world, poached turtle eggs were the toughest to get down.

In all these things, however, I manage to submit to various cultural authorities by the grace of God and the love in the eyes of the people who offered their best to me. I have heard man speak in a hundred different languages, met him over vast continents and in the darkest, strangest places of the world. I've watched him strive with all his heart to harmonize with the spirit of God prevalent in nature, and to care for those around him. In all my travels, I have learned one vital thread uniting us all. Be it in the pure eyes of the young or the weathered eyes of the old, love is unmistakable. Because of love, I can eat a dozen turtle eggs and drink spit beer until I'm reciting Swahili poetry. I can travel upriver in a ramshackle canoe while piranhas nip at the gunwales, ravenous for my flesh. I can walk for hours through a sweltering jungle while my hosts lead me to an ailing woman needing prayer. I can do all these things and more through our Savior who loves us.

Covenant Authority

Covenant authority, the last in this discussion, is simply the authority of an agreement. When people make an agreement, the binding force of that agreement carries an authority.

Like many people, I like to do business relationally. When I take my truck in to the garage for an oil change or brake job, I know who will be working on it because I have spent time with them. I've listened to their stories. I've gotten to know them. The person replacing my muffler is not merely a "mechanic." It's Joe Burns, or Elizabeth Walton, or Hank Lester. You see, people buy from people. I'm not dealing with an institution or a corporation or even a local grease pit. I'm dealing with living, thinking, feeling human beings, and it is with these beings that I form covenants.

I have a 23-year relationship with one of my mechanics. He is not perfect but he is a good mechanic and I trust him. Because of covenant authority, I know that the work I require will be done right, and my mechanic knows that if something extra needs to be done, he has the authority to do it. He has done major work on our vehicles—the very cars and trucks that Susan and I use to carry us to ministry engagements. Most people would not look at a greasy mechanic and think: *Oh, he's in ministry.* But he is. Without that mechanic and the trust that binds us together, I wouldn't get far in reaching the world with the gospel.

Similarly, if I call a local car dealer that I know, and say that I will be over to pick up a certain vehicle, they will start the paperwork and prepare the car on the authority of our agreement. At the same time, I expect them to honor their word to sell it to me at the agreed upon price. In both instances, we are operating in the authority of covenant established by our word.

Covenant authority is felt the strongest when an agreement is difficult to fulfill. I have made arrangements with people in one frame of heart, and later when it came time to deliver my part, I found that my energy levels had shifted and the resources I was expecting to carry out my promise were no longer available. In most cases, I find a way to honor my word. In very rare instances, after doing everything in my power to complete the agreement, I will go to the person with whom I have the agreement and ask to be released.

Covenant carries authority; it is empowered by grace and bound by mercy.

Chapter 7

Relationships

Relationship governs our shared reality with another person.

Influence

Authority gets things done. Yes it does! But the other side of the coin is that it takes people to get things done. Authority, therefore, is how we influence people. And the relationship between authority and people is just that: *relationships*.

Relationships

A person's most powerful, life-shaping experiences come from their relationships.

Talk with anyone on a personal level, and if you listen carefully, you will hear a familiar theme. You will hear about issues with their mother, their father, their children, their friends, their workmates, their church, their boss, their distant relatives, and of course, their spouses. You will hear what was said, what was done, what was meant by what was said and done, and how the speaker's words and actions were interpreted. You will discover how each of these interactions influences the speaker's life, and how relationships govern their shared reality with others. Eventually, the conversation will reveal an interwoven fabric—the tapestry of their life.

Authority and Relationship

Authentic authority is relational. It works through relationship to influence people. Without relationship, I will not willingly accept someone's authority, and so, they cannot influence me. The quality of relationship I have with another determines how much they can influence me. Through relationship, their authority can influence me only as far as our shared trust, knowledge, and experience. For example, my wife can influence me at a deep level; my friends can influence me at a moderate level, and my neighbors can influence me at a light level. Because I am in a different relationship with all three people groups, their authority in my life is different and consequently, they influence me differently.

Similarly, I find that in ministry, my ability to influence others is governed by how we relate to one another. The most powerful question in a ministerial relationship is: *Who am I to you?* The answer to that question governs my ability to influence the person.

In World War II, General Patton led hundreds of thousands of soldiers into battle. They followed his orders because he was their general. However, the rest of the nation did not follow Patton into battle. He was not their leader. They did not see him as their general. They saw him differently. Congress, for example, saw a subordinate. The military-industrial complex saw a customer. Average citizens saw a war hero. And Mrs. Patton saw a driven man who occasionally visited home and forgot to put his dirty socks in the laundry.

Obviously, relationships are important to accomplishing things, but how do they work? How do they develop? And how do they affect the work of God today? We will answer these questions by looking at the stages of relationships and their influence.

Relationships and their influence fall into five categories:

- Positional

- Preferred

- Purposeful

- Developmental

- Relational Covenant

These categories represent a progression of influence from the weakest to the strongest, from the least effective to the most powerful. In examining each type, we will draw from the Bible examples of people and places that illustrate particular relationship characteristics. On our way, we will visit the Cave of Adullam, Hebron, Ziklag, and Zion. We will learn that:

- Adullam is a place of deliverance.

- Ziklag is a place of unity.

- Hebron is a place of development.

- Zion is a place of deployment and being one with God.

Our goal is to reach the place of deployment through relational covenant, the deepest and most powerful level of relationship.

Chapter 8

Positional Authority

A leader is someone who...

Bitter of Soul

L et us begin our journey to relational covenant at the Cave of Adullam, and examine positional authority—the authority in which many ministries function today. From the early life of David, we read of his escape from King Saul, the despot desperately trying to kill him:

> *David therefore departed from there and escaped to the cave of Adullam. So when his brothers and all his father's house heard it, they went down there to him. And everyone who was in distress, everyone who was in debt, and everyone who was discontented gathered to him. So he became captain over them. And there were about four hundred men with him.*
>
> 1 Samuel 22:1-2

To evade the pursuing armies of Saul, David hid in the cave of Adullam. I imagine he felt pretty lonely hiding in a damp, cold cave with water dripping from the ceiling, each plop counting the minutes, hours, and days he'd spent there contemplating a dark and dismal future. The Psalms from that time reveal a man of desperation, though not without hope. David had been the hero of the kingdom after slaying Goliath, but here he was fleeing for his life without a friend in sight...until now. Turns out that other people were fleeing Saul as well. The worst thing Saul ever did for himself was to oppress so many people that they formed an army.

These people saw in David a rallying point, a sympathetic hero, a man they could gather around and develop into a unifying force. The fact that David was also fleeing Saul gave him authenticity. The people could relate to his position. They were oppressed and running from Saul; David was also oppressed and running from Saul. Moreover, the people wished to be victorious over Saul. David had already scored a victory over Saul when he rose in fame after slaying Goliath. Misery loves company, and David's company was plenty miserable when they found him and threw in their lot with him.

Remember our definition of a leader: *A leader is someone who can take you to a place you don't desire to go and cause you to discover you have purpose there.* The people gathering around David were seeking purpose—in this case, to escape the ravages of Saul's corrupt kingdom and find a better life.

The fact that David's father, brothers, and other community members also gathered to him is significant considering that David was the reject of the family. Most Bible scholars accept that David was illegitimate—the offspring of an illicit affair. Further, he was relegated to the lowest duty of the family—shepherd. He was not even considered when Samuel came to anoint one of his brothers (Jesse's sons). In spite of all these disadvantages, however, those who were distressed, in debt, and discontent—*bitter of soul* is the exact translation—were drawn to David's authority, and he became a captain to them.

Now, obviously a cave is not the best place to live long-term. During a harsh winter, it might do in a pinch, but it is not luxurious surroundings. Yet the people who gathered around David were not looking for comfort; they wanted deliverance from all that was afflicting them. They saw David as one who inhabited the same place as they did but who had the ability to defeat Saul. They related to him positionally, and he became a captain to them. In turn, David provided deliverance. Through the authority that arose from this positional relationship, he began to lead them safely away from Saul's oppression and gathered them under a new banner: that of his (and God's) future kingdom.

Authentic authority can take someone who is in debt, distressed, or bitter of soul, and bring them to a place of deliverance, even when the journey is uncomfortable. This is why Adullam is a place of deliverance. God used David to deliver those who needed help. David saw their need, accepted their allegiance, exercised authentic authority, and rose up as their leader. He did all these things at the level of positional relationship.

However, as we shall see later, we can experience a move of God in the place of deliverance, but it will not sustain us. I can throw a robber out of your house, but unless you buy better locks, fortify your abode, or move to a better neighborhood, the robber will come back. Jesus told us this with respect to spiritual deliverance:

"When an unclean spirit goes out of a man, he goes through dry places, seeking rest, and finds none. Then he says, 'I will return to my house from which I came.' And when he comes, he finds it empty, swept, and put in order. Then he goes and takes with him

seven other spirits more wicked than himself, and they enter and dwell there; and the last state of that man is worse than the first.

Matthew 12:43-45

Yes, deliverance is important. But the true, lasting move of God cannot be completed in the Cave of Adullam.

Positional Relationship

From the Cave of Adullam, David operated in positional relationship with his people, meaning that the people submitted to his authority based on his position or title. Adullam became a place of deliverance for distressed people, formed under a person of authority, a person they thought they knew. But did they really know David? Intimately? Or was it simply his hero status—and now his refugee status—that made him a leader they could rally around and find strength in through numbers?

The people who gathered under David did not know him; they only knew *of* him. They knew his great deeds, his acts of courage, his reputation, and ultimately, his position as a rebel leader. They saw his position, knew his title, and accepted his authority, but they did not know the man. Nor did he know them. Still, it was a start.

Positional relationships are where most Christian organizations start today. At this level, people will follow leadership because of a title or position. A person will follow a pastor, prophet, teacher, or apostle based on the title and the energy emanating forth. That is how they relate to the ministry and how they accept influence from the minister.

Now, positional relationships are alright for some people… for a while. Many—especially those seeking deliverance—are not looking for deep relationship in their lives, at least, not right away.

Instead, they are seeking to be associated with something bigger than themselves, a title or organization that evokes the security and success that is missing from their personal lives. The authority they relate to in these cases is a distant, impersonal authority. It can't touch where they really live because they won't let it get that close.

Sadly, because *authentic authority is relational*, they are rejecting deeper, meaningful relationships as well. We can't have an intimate relationship with a title, a position, or an organization. Real relationships are made with real people under real circumstances. But like those who gathered under David, positional authority and the influence it engenders is a place to start.

I have seen people at the positional level encounter God in dramatic ways: slain in the spirit, receive heart-rending prophecies, healed inside and out. Yet without maturing into deeper levels of relationship, they fail to hold on to the benefits of those experiences. The touch of God that made them whole is soon lost to the same cross-currents of flesh and darkness that were drowning them before God arrived.

A Rose By Any Other Name

Many people under the ministry God gave me will submit to my authority because they relate to me as a pastor, teacher, or apostle. And I know they benefit from doing so. But I've also learned that we can never really develop a life-giving relationship based on a position or title. Eventually, we need more.

Relationships are not made in heaven. They are made down here in the tough and dirty. Like the garden that man was commissioned to cultivate, relationships must be nurtured in the soil of our lives. Life comes at us fast. There are things and people that let us down despite the best of intentions, and yet these are the best times for relationship building. Positional relationships will not carry us through the hard times; personal relationships will.

At a positional level, as people follow leadership because of a title, the influence in their lives from that ministry will not extend beyond their superficial understanding of the job description.

I find that there are four things that people call me in our church (at least to my face). They call me: *Apostle, Brother Clay, Pastor*, or *Poppa*. I don't have a problem with these titles or the functions they imply, except perhaps for *Pastor*. This is because I am not a pastor; I know how to pastor, but it is not in line with my primary anointing flow. Of course, I understand what people mean when they use the term, and more so, I sense what they are drawing from me as they apply the term, so I don't mind when they call me *Pastor*. But they will eventually migrate to the influence of others within our body whose primary gifting aligns closer with that of a pastor.

Now, those who refer to me as *Apostle* are typically looking for more—the leadership that an apostle of God can bring to their lives. This, through God's Spirit, is what I am able to provide them. However, while the people who call me *Brother Clay* will always get the best I can give them, I know I can never be their leader because they are not looking for leadership; they are looking for a peer. Yes, I can show them where to feed; I can get them to the right pasture; I can encourage them; I can even drive the enemy from their lives. But I can never turn them into a mighty warrior under a peer to peer relationship.

The reason many people fail to grow under a ministry is that they think that relating to the position or title *is* true relationship. It's not. If they can't get the relationship right, they won't be able to draw on the minister's anointing. Conversely, if the minister only relates to others on the basis of his or her title and position, the Spirit of God will be hindered as they minister. My anointing flows best when I am in relationship with a person—the real person. Authentic authority and influence flows through relationship.

Imagine two cups: one is full and one is empty. To pour from the full one into the empty one, I have to position the empty one lower than the full one for a time. In life, when we submit to authority, we can draw from that authority and are influenced by it. Remember: authority is our friend. God placed it in our lives for a reason.

Those who gathered to David knew he had something they needed, and they honored him by accepting him as captain. This enabled David's life—his spirit, his wisdom, his insight, his strength—to flow to their areas of need. Sharing the same life, they began to unite into an effective army. Eventually, they moved from positional relationships into something greater. They were joining together under David himself, partaking of more than his fame or charisma. They began to share of his spirit and bonded with his life.

In contrast, when groups are based solely on following positions and titles, they experience a high rate of turnover. People arrive, are eager for a while, but eventually they fail to bond with those around them, so they leave searching for something more. This is because people inherently sense that their deep needs are not being fulfilled under positional relationships. Tragically, they think that the particular ministerial position they have committed to following is not adequate, or not the right one, so they move on to another, only to find the same results. What they need to realize is that the fault does not lie with the position; it lies in focusing *on* the position. When we relate to the very people whom God has set in our lives for leadership, all goes well with us.

Higher and Higher

After the fervent days of the early church, formal religion gradually replaced authentic authority while positional relationships formed the new foundation. This resulted in a terrible wall of separation between clergy and laity. One telling sign of this division was the position of pulpits in churches. As the relational distance between ministers and their people grew, pulpits were gradually elevated from the church floor to higher and higher perches. It was from these lofty lecterns that the spiritually impoverished were addressed, admonished, and absolved—at least for another week. How easy to dictate "truth" to the flock while remaining relationally insulated at nosebleed elevations.

It is at this point that I must relate an old axiom that I heard years ago. *The higher the monkey climbs up the flag pole, the more you can see his posterior.* (That's not *quite* how I heard it, but you get the gist.) Aloof ministers wrapped in protective behaviors are advertising far and wide their raging insecurity and personality flaws. They are up there for a reason. *What are you afraid of? Shimmy on down here and learn to relate as a redeemed human being. We can see you anyway.*

In the churches I am associated with, we move the pulpits down on the floor for a very good reason. People must understand that we are ministering to them from the same level—physically and relationally. If I am on level ground with my people, they are going to be more willing to submit their hearts to my anointing, and I am going to be more inclined to be real in return. Because of this, the power of God will flow unhindered.

The truth of Jesus needs no help from the flesh of man. Truth stands wherever we are open, authentic, humble, honest, and willing before God and man. Notice that "perfect" did not make the list.

Relationships Across the Altar

We must work hard to tear down the separation between clergy and laity. It is a positional viewpoint that kills relationship rather than grows it.

In Latin, *laity* means *someone who is unable to learn*—in the vernacular: *an idiot.* What an unfortunate connotation, as it puts down the congregation and falsely lifts up the ministerial staff. Faced with this definition, most people would deny that such a separation even exists. And yet, that is exactly the condition we have in many churches. Either you have a title before your name, or you are nobody. And how do we come into this tragic arrangement? Obviously, by focusing on the position rather than the person.

Of course, it goes both ways. While people attempt to draw from a minister by virtue of their title or position, many in ministry attempt to give to others *through* their title or position. And this can work...for a while. I have seen people blessed who only related to the title of the person ministering. This is because fundamentally, people can receive anything that God wants to give them, provided they have the faith to receive and hold it. However, it cannot last.

The key to ministering positionally is for the minister to never, ever, *ever* let the congregation see him as he really is. The wall of separation that starts with people's focus on a title must be perpetuated by the minister hiding behind that same wall. As the parishioners reinforce the barrier from one side with their misdirected focus, the minister must shore it up from the other side to ward off unwanted intrusion and continue the masquerade. *Pay no attention to that man behind the curtain!* Some Bible schools actually teach their students—future ministers of God—to not get personally close to their people because they might become too familiar. And familiarity, as we all know, breeds contempt.

I feel just the opposite. I want to get close to my people because when they see my flaws, they will pray for me, support me, and even teach me a thing or two. We all have flaws; there is not a person alive, nor a church in existence, without flaws. God is into perfecting things. However, he does not demand perfection. While perfection is the goal that puts us on a journey, it is the journey that causes us to grow. Ministers must realize that they are on the same journey as their people.

The problems I've described above can grow especially acute when the person in ministry entered it seeking personal identity and fulfillment. The truth is that no title can give us self-worth. If it could, Jesus would simply title each one of us when we get saved: *Lord Smith, Lady Elaine, His Majesty Mike.* Instead, he gave each of us *HIS* name, *HIS* spirit, and *HIS* identity. Our identity, regardless of our title, must be that of sons of God.

That will just have to do, I reckon.

Chapter 9

Preferred Relationships

I'm outta here is not a solution to life's challenges.

Preferred Relationship

From the story of David and his journey to the Cave of Adullam, we see an interesting development. The very people who originally related to him positionally began to develop into the mighty men and women who formed the core of his army and eventual kingdom. Obviously they were moving from positional relationships to something more, growing in allegiance to David and to one another.

The second progression on our journey to a relational covenant is preferred relationship. At this level of influence, people will follow leaders because they prefer one over another.

When people influence us, it can be in a good way, a bad way, or somewhere in between. Like most people, I find negative influences to be draining. When I'm around negative people, I get tired quicker, become discouraged easier, and soon find myself questioning why I even ride a Harley in the first place considering all the great motorcycles that Honda makes. That's when I know I'm in trouble.

So I exercise my preference in relationships whenever possible. Yes, at times, we all have to be around certain people who make us wish we were somewhere else. But given the choice, I prefer to be around positive people, and prefer *not* to be around negative people.

The people I prefer to associate with energize me; they stimulate me and infuse me with life. More so, they point me to the Savior in an honest, open, and vital way. They are upfront about my faults as well as my sterling qualities, and they are open to my input as well. These are life-giving relationships.

Life is contagious. Healthy people prefer to be around those who influence them in healthy ways. They don't want to be around complainers, whiners, or perpetual victims. As we grow in maturity, it is not that we don't tolerate difficult people. In fact, we are to love them, reach out to them, and care for them. Eventually, many of them will come to the light of Jesus that they (hopefully) see within us. But given the choice, who do we prefer to spend our quality time with? Obviously, we have our preferences.

Preferred relationships are a step up from positional relationships, but they are not always sustainable. Through preferred relationships, we accept and can give a greater level of authority, resulting in a deeper influence. But at this level of influence, people will follow leaders because they choose to. And as good as preferred influence can be, it only goes so far. This is because the decision to participate in a preferred relationship is out of preference and not out of conviction. Why is conviction important? Let's look at this closer.

Preference and Conviction

When Cain and Abel brought their offerings before the Lord, Cain brought his offering because he preferred to bring it. Abel brought a more excellent offering because he was convicted by God to do so. Unfortunately, Cain's offering was rejected, and as we all know, he took it rather personally.

Many people today attend churches out of preference: they like the worship, enjoy the sermon, and think the doughnuts in the lobby are great. Yet, while they enjoy the positive, uplifting atmosphere, they are still not there out of a conviction that God wants them there. As such, they are not likely to stick around when things get tough. If the worship team undergoes a transition, if the sermons suddenly tank, or if the hospitality team switches from junk food to fresh fruit trays, these folks will be rushing the exits. Yes, it is great when people choose to associate with positive moves of God's Spirit, but where is the staying power? Preferred relationships are an interim step, but they are not the goal.

Marriage Conviction

When we get married, we usually do so because we prefer the other person. However, we soon learn that preference alone will not maintain—let alone grow—a marriage.

When I was married at 20 years of age, I thought I knew everything and my dad knew nothing. Let me tell you something. In the first three years of marriage, my dad must have enrolled in night school or something. Lord gracious! How he grew in wisdom in such a short time. The things he had told me about marriage were right on, but I couldn't hear them because I wasn't paying attention. My dad understood the fallacies of trying to live married life through preferred influence. Experience had taught him that to build relationship, it takes something more than a preference that can be present one day and gone the next. It takes the conviction that you belong there, that nothing will uproot you, and that you are in it for the long haul.

In the early years of our marriage, I was not the easiest cat to herd, but what kept us together was the understanding that something more than preference holds people in relationships over the hard times.

Preferred influence is rooted in immaturity. When people are operating in preferred influence, it becomes painfully obvious during difficult circumstances. When the lights of our rosy outlook dim, our first instinct is to flee the dysfunction—anything but hang in there and grow. Of course, there is nothing wrong with immaturity as long as we recognize it and move on from there.

What Dad Required

I learned early on that Dad required more of me than what preferred influence would provide.

My Dad and I had several businesses before I married Susan, and although I could draw money from them, I never did. I never took a dime until I married Susan in 1973. Even though I worked for Dad every week—some weeks were 100 hours—I never accepted a paycheck. Instead, Dad paid all my bills and gave me a little spending money. I always had money in my pocket, and I always worked hard. He was wise never to give me too much money back then; I'd have only gotten in trouble with it. Instead, he kept pouring the capital back into the businesses to make them grow. That is wisdom.

Being the restless sort, I bought my first pickup truck when I was 13 years old. I paid $350 for it; $25 down and Dad financed the rest for me. I didn't have a license yet, but occasionally Dad would let me sneak down some back roads and practice driving on the farm.

Now, in Arkansas back in 1966, it was possible to get a hardship license at age 13—meaning that you needed to drive on a limited basis in order to help support your family. However, an interesting thing happened when I applied for my license. People today will find this strange, but when I took my driver's test, they did not ask for a birth certificate. So I simply filled in my birthday, but when I wrote 1953, for some reason (possibly my poor penmanship), my driver's license came back showing me born in 1950. So at 13 years of age, I suddenly became 16. Of course, my dad loved it because it meant that he could take me anywhere he wanted to. He also trusted me to drive by then, and now that I was legal (technically), I could run errands for him all over the state in my new (to me) truck.

It was not always smooth sailing with my Dad, however. All that summer, I mowed yards in order to make my $25 a month truck payment to him. Then October came around, the lawn care business dried up, and I could not make my next payment. No problem, I was his son. Family bestows certain inalienable rights, and financial forgiveness is chief among them, right? Well, that's what I'd always read. Unfortunately, my Dad and I didn't read the same books.

The instant the payment was late, Dad repossessed my truck. He did not wait until I was three months behind, no sir. He took the keys right out of my pocket, parked the truck out front of the house, and left me with an ultimatum. *"If you don't catch up on your payments in 30 days, a For Sale sign is going in the window and she'll be gone."*

As a boy of 13, in love with his first set of wheels, I was devastated.

Now, if this would have happened in today's environment, I would have called Child Welfare, had Dad arrested, then I would have received counseling for my damaged ego and been placed in a foster home until Dad relented and gave me his truck for free, or until my new family bought me a Porsche. But this was Arkansas in 1966, and I was faced with a stark reality—give up the truck, or find a way to make my payments. It was at this point that my bruised psyche had an epiphany: the end of grass-cutting season meant the beginning of leaf-falling season. Glory to God who made all these trees! I ended up earning a fortune raking leaves, cleaning gutters, trimming trees, and helping elderly ladies across busy streets. (Just kidding on the elderly ladies—I never charged for that.) I made enough that fall to pay for my truck. And thanks to my traumatic experience 45 years ago, I've never missed another truck payment.

Responsibility builds maturity and maturity requires more than preferred influence. That's what Dad taught me. That's what leaders do. This is what Jesus expects us to become as we journey to relational covenants.

Here For Hear

In preferred relationships, receiving counsel from leaders is easy as long as they give us the counsel we want. This is why some people go from counselor to counselor until they find the person who tells them it is OK to do what they want to do. If we search long enough, we can find someone to support our preferences for anything.

Like Cain, when we do things because we prefer to do them and not because we are convicted to do them, there is little faith involved. Anything we do for God—communion, water baptism, offerings, praise, or witnessing—if we don't release faith as we do it, it can easily become a ritual rooted in death and embalmed with unbelief.

After Cain despised his brother and murdered him, God spoke a curse over him, saying he was going to be a vagabond. What's a vagabond? A hobo, a traveler, someone with no place to hang their hat, no place to call home. God told Cain he would be a vagabond on the earth with no rest for the soles of his feet. If we remain operating in preferred influence, we run the risk of ending up just as Cain did: no home, no relationships, a curse upon the earth.

Please note that I say *remain operating in....* We all journey through preferred relationships. It is Holy Spirit's job to take us through this journey. However, we can't stop. We are not here to camp, build houses, and remain in preferred influence any more than we are to remain in the third grade. Preferred relationships are a way station towards greater relationships. It is as if God is saying to us, *"Glad you found something you like, now let's talk about making a real commitment to it."*

Vagabond Church

As we consider the realities of relating to others on a deeper level, we must face the fact that the charismatic church is full of vagabonds—people who flourish for a time, then get offended (it's bound to happen eventually) and deal with it by pulling up stakes to find another church...or no church at all.

Of course, some people leave congregations in peace. As a leader, I know that it hurts to lose good people. But sometimes it's time to move on, and I know that wherever God directs these people, they will enter the next place in peace. For these, I bless them and stay in contact with them.

Yet departures are not always handled that well. Most times, I see people leave houses of God upset, resentful, and full of venom. They don't leave in peace, and sadly, they can't enter into the next place in peace. I see a vagabond spirit over the body of Christ—predominately among the charismatic people.

Charismatic churches are all for spiritual liberty; we believe we can do anything we want. But while this opens many doors for Holy Spirit to move, it is also fertile ground for operating solely in preference. Because of preferred relationships, we easily take on the attitude that we are here as long as it suits us.

In our network of churches, we have had many come to us based on our reputation. They stay for a while and then they move on, citing some incident or experience that ran counter to their expectations. Frankly, it breaks my heart to see them leave. But I have to wonder what brought them in the first place. If true conviction brought them, then conviction would have kept them. I can only pray that their journey through preferred influence and on to relational covenants continues, and that they find peace in maturity at the next place they land.

Still, we have had others come with a firm conviction that this is where they were to serve. God moved them here and God kept them here. I know people who have left good jobs to join our congregations. I am honored by these, and our benevolence flows towards those who operate from the deep well of conviction.

The Enemy Strikes Back

We see how important conviction is by the way the enemy attacks that area. When Holy Spirit begins moving, Satan is sure to stir people's hearts in opposition, and one of the first areas to be exploited is conviction...specifically, the lack thereof.

I saw this clearly one time when I ministered in a Midwest church. It was the first time I was there. I was asked to come by a senior apostle who shepherded that church. Now, the first time I minister to a congregation, I try to be on my best behavior. I like to feel the place out and stay within the apparent boundaries. Of course, God can have other ideas.

The Saturday night that I first ministered, I felt the Spirit fall with a mighty WOOSH! God showed up, miracles started happening, healings and prophecies were everywhere—it was overwhelming. I came back Sunday morning and it was a repeat of the night before. The absolute glory of God came into that place with signs and wonders shaking the foundation. I'm telling you, it got scary.

Then on Monday morning, the bottom fell out. The worship leader, who had been with the church for many years, came to the senior minister and announced that he was resigning and taking every influential family in the church with him. Apparently, the move of God was not what these people were expecting—they preferred something different, and they intended to find it...somewhere else. Of course, the church survived and even flourished. We took them into our network of fellowship and they are thriving today. However, note the area that the enemy attacked: the conviction of the foundational members.

The enemy does not want us in the will of God. Tests and trials are going to come but we have to keep pressing in beyond them. To do so, we must move past a preferred relational mindset. Please burn this into your conscience: _I'm outta here_ is not a solution to life's challenges. Most of the time, it means the enemy is removing you from something good that God wants for your life. Yes, people come and go, and God moves people here and there. The distinction is the spirit in which we move. Are we leaving under the benediction of the single digit, or are we moving onward and upward in the joy of the Lord? The sure signs of God's moving are whether we are maturing every time we move on, and what awaits us when we get there. The distinction is preference versus conviction.

The Journey

Yes, preferred influence is part of the journey, but we must progress beyond it. Followers will only remain in a relationship of preferred influence with leaders who provide what they want. When preference brings people into a ministry, they can just as easily prefer to leave anytime they like. But if they are convicted to be there, they can't change it. They can run from a conviction, but they can't hide from it. Not even a big, smelly whale can shield someone from the call of God on their heart.

Naturally, many people don't want to pay the price of conviction—at least, not right away. A relational covenant is not established immediately. It takes time. We are all maturing; we are all growing.

When people join a congregation, they are seeking, evaluating, judging and trying to hear God in that place. Trust must be established. Credibility must demonstrate a proven track record. Authority must be exhibited within the love of God. These assurances are not always present the instant you meet a person, encounter a ministry, or join a body of believers. Remember our key word in our studies: *Journey*. No, not a rock band from California, but a progression that God has us all on. Along the way, people can get hurt by poor leadership, and because of this, they expect the next leader to hurt them as well. Our journey is one of finding truth and healing. As confidence is cultivated, people will reach for God in the areas to which he is leading them.

As an apostle, I realize that I carry a big stick. Yet if I ever have to speak correction into a person's life, it is because I value them. In my years of ministry, I have learned to recognize those who will receive correction from those who will not. I know this from the level of influence that I have in their lives. Those who are seeking God and have a measure of trust in my anointing will accept words of correction. Others will turn a deaf ear, become offended, and will probably leave, doing their best to take others with them. I know to leave those people alone. I pray for them—they are on the same journey we all are on—just not as far along.

But for those who can accept my influence, here is the blessing. By receiving God's word, they mature into a whole new level of grace. They grow in the areas where correction is applied. Consequently, they step into a new area of strength where instruction by me is no longer required. We flow in harmony, and subtle hints of discord are all that is required for us to adjust pitch.

Right Motives/Wrong Results

People who are highly motivated but remain at the level of preferred influence become easily restless. If they relate to a minister out of position or preference, they will eventually consider moving when it appears that the church down the street is bigger, more active, and able to help them achieve what they want. Oftentimes, it is a bigger platform to continue their own ministry.

While there is nothing wrong with ambition, if the ambitious person doesn't mature beyond preference, he or she will eventually become rebellious. All that pent-up energy has to go somewhere; when thwarted, it can lead to some frustrated acting-out. Other than the immediate difficulties that rebellion presents, it also removes a person further from the very influences that are needed to mature them beyond preference. So by running, the person is perpetuating the forces driving his or her negative behavior.

> *Where there is no revelation, the people cast off restraint; but happy is he who keeps the law.*

> Proverbs 29:18

Years ago I had a man help me start a church. He had an incredible administration gift, and I grew to appreciate him tremendously. Yet he kept asking to preach. So, despite my better judgment, I gave him the pulpit several times. Trouble was, every time I did, terrible things happened. People got up and walked out; they fell asleep; they came back later and wanted to argue over the sermon. It soon became apparent that this man was not called to preach. When I finally set him down and shared my observations, I became the scourge of the earth in his eyes. He and his family left in a fury and I have not seen him since. I did send him a friend request about 3 years ago, and as of this writing, I am still not his friend. (The ultimate rejection in our modern culture, I guess.)

Now, I wish this story was unique to my ministry, but it is not. Instead, it is played out in churches everywhere. People get offended, hold a grudge, and close the door to any further contact. I have had people refuse to have anything to do with a ministry that is associated with another ministry that once had a preacher who referred to another preacher who hurt those people 30 years ago. (Whew!) Certainly, no ministry is perfect, and pain will make people do strange things, but I have a prophetic word of healing for those in such bondage: *Grow up and get over it!*

I began learning this lesson as a boy. In school (45 years ago), a coach gave me a licking with a size 16 tennis shoe for something I didn't do. Now, by today's standards, this would have landed him in jail. But this was then; standards were different. Every time he swatted me, it brought me off the floor. It hurt vividly. Through my sobs, I tried to tell him I was not the one who did it. I was not lying; I really did not do it. In fact, the guy who did do it came up later and confessed. So it was outright injustice, and it hurt. Man, did it hurt. (Have I mentioned that it was not particularly pleasant?)

Soon after that, my mother and father divorced. I was devastated, and that same coach with the size 16 tennis shoe saw my emotional carnage and took me under his wing. At the time, I was about 5 foot 4, 12 years of age, and he worked with me every day on the basketball court, encouraging me and listening to me. Did the licking hurt? Oh my gracious; I could not sit for two days. Was the man perfect? Not by a country mile. But I learned to value who he was. He made a mistake, but he was also the one who God used to pull me through a very tough time.

How long can we carry offenses? How long are we going to remember them? We have to let these offenses go. They cover our wounds, prevent our healing, and stunt our growth. We can't get better by hating the people or institutions that hurt us. Offenses take our eyes off the very things that God brings into our life to help us.

Chapter 10

Purposeful Relationships

All authority is influence, but not all influence is authority.

Hebron

We saw from the Cave of Adullam that afflicted people gathered to David on the basis of positional relationship and preferred relationship. We find the same to be true today; churches are full of people sick at heart and needing deliverance in some form or fashion. However, while many want to be delivered by God, fewer want to be deployed into the place of their true destiny. This reluctance is normal—regrettable, but normal. It also explains why Jesus ministered one way to the masses, and a different way to those closest to him. He saved his most intimate teaching for those seeking to go further in ministry, to the glory of God. Some people only seek and appreciate the things of God. Others, as they mature, seek out God himself—how they might know him and serve him. This is the progression of relational maturation.

To further understand the process of maturation, we must leave the Cave of Adullam and focus on a place called Hebron, which becomes our place of purposeful development. We haven't totally dealt with the issues that drove us to the cave, but as we address our debt, our discontentment, and our bitterness of soul, we will begin to reach out for maturity and placement within the Body of Christ.

Geographically, Mount Hebron, in Israel, is one of the highest points of elevation in the Middle East. According to legend, people traveled to Hebron by a place called Ziklag. The word *Ziklag* in the Hebrew means winding, treacherous trail. It snakes up a 1,000 foot, narrow ledge cut into a rock cliff. The only way to get to Hebron during Bible days was along that sliver of ledge with your back against the rock wall, shuffling your feet from side to side. For survival, people tied themselves together—moving when the group moved, and catching each other if one of them slipped and fell. You had to hope that fewer people fell than who remained. This is one reason that the Bible says to not be unequally yoked with unbelievers.

To get to the physical Hebron, people had to learn to work together. To get to the spiritual Hebron today—the place of development—people *still* have to learn to work together. *Can two walk together unless they agree?* (Amos 3:3) If one of us slips and falls, the strength of our bond one to another will pull that one up.

In the spirit, Hebron is where we learn to walk together and work together. We become yoked and develop a team effort. When one falls, it hurts everybody. When one stands, it helps everybody. Teamwork is more than an option; our survival depends on it. It doesn't take long to realize that each of us falls at some point, and it is our relational bonds that restore us.

Of course, one might ask why people made the journey to Hebron at all. If it was so treacherous back then, why bother? The reason people have always made the journey of that winding treacherous trail to Hebron is that, as one of the highest points in the land, and you can look out and see Zion—the place of God's relational covenant with man.

Adullam is a place of deliverance; Hebron is a place of development. And what do we develop? The ability to move together. The ability to trust each other. Teamwork. Unity.

Unity

Now, unity is easy to say but more difficult to achieve. Part of the problem is that we tend to distrust anyone who is different from ourselves. This is unfortunate. The body of Christ needs to grow beyond the human instinct to only bond with those who are similar to us. We tend to disassociate with people who look different, act different, or think different. God made us unique, but he also made us similar. When people bond, they actually form the strongest bonds at the point of their greatest personal differences, for our differences highlight one person's strengths and another's weaknesses. In a word: we bond over our *needs*.

You might ask where I learned this. Then again, I just might tell you anyway. Like most people, I struggle with those who are different than I am. Being a southern male, I am used to an outdoor lifestyle of hunting, horses, camping and motorcycles, so I don't always bond immediately with other types of people—namely those who think the movie *Bambi* was a documentary. But I have learned that I need all kinds of people in my life more than I need those who are like me. Sure, I have my hunting buddies who talk like me, walk like me, and shoot like me (straight). But it is the people who aren't like me who challenge me, expose my foibles and prejudices, edit my books and ultimately cause me to grow.

Even different ministers appeal to different people. In our spiritual house, I am known for a more ad-hoc style of preaching; it fits my personality and my spiritual giftings. But we have others in our church who are more measured, orderly, and predictable. And that style appeals to many people. I praise God for the differences between ministers among us, because it means that even more people will be reached and encouraged to respond to the Spirit's leading.

Dance Like a Spinning Top

I knew a man named Fred who used to dance in church. He loved God, I could see that clearly, but he was a bit effeminate. Fred liked to dance with his pinky up in the air, spinning and twirling as you would expect a woman to dance. Now, to my frame of mind, men don't dance like that. We might stomp our foot, we might shake our heads, but it's more of a war dance than a ballet. So I gave Fred his space and he gave me mine.

One night during service, as I was trying to focus on the Lord and ignore everyone else, I decided to raise my hands to at least look like I'm worshiping in the spirit. Well, here comes Fred, swirling down the aisle while the worship music played, and somehow by the grace of God (*I'll blame it on God*) Fred's hand bumped mine. Of course, I jumped a little. But then I felt something change—a transfer of anointing. Suddenly my whole viewpoint on dancing in church shifted radically. I had a new freedom of expression, a greater confidence to move, and I found myself stepping into worship in a deeper way. This effeminate man who danced like a girl and probably never shot a buck in his life had just imparted to me the true spirit of dancing before the Lord. Resplendent in my western boots, jeans and cowboy hat, I began to twirl down the aisle right behind Fred.

Somebody who was radically different from me completely changed my life that night. The following week, I brought Fred a nice venison steak.

Purpose

We find in Hebron the need for greater authority than the positional or preferred relationships of Adullam can provide. This is because, as we develop, our need for greater unity will require a strong influencing force to bind us together. In our journey towards development, we must begin to form purposeful relationships. At the level of purposeful relationship, people will follow a ministry based on what they see being accomplished. Moreover, in purposeful relationships, we see a certain amount of relational covenant and we begin to establish relational authority, but we are not there yet.

Authentic, life-giving authority flows through relationship, establishing trust as we choose to trust. Without relationship, people are not going to allow a ministry to influence their lives. Remember our illustration of the pulpits in the middle-ages being placed higher and higher above the people? The authority in those churches hurt more people than it helped. The more remote the minister, the more death reigned over the people. When I can't relate to a person, I can't receive from a person—not in the life-giving Spirit of God.

All authority is influence, but not all influence is authority.

People are drawn to purpose. They love to be a part of a vibrant movement. In churches, we want to be where the action is: miracles, healings, salvations, and outreach. In business, people like being part of start-up companies engaged in developing and marketing ground-breaking technologies like levitating trains, super-conductors, and mining asteroids. In the arts, people thrive on the cutting edge of artistic expression, the vanguard of exploration: a stark ivory canvas with a single slash of red; an entire orchestra sitting still for 15 minutes; a 6 hour film of nothing but the Empire State Building.

As I said earlier, people love to work with Richard Branson, the entrepreneur who founded Virgin Group which operates several airlines and has been wildly successful. He owns over 400 companies, among them Virgin Air, Virgin Train and Virgin Telephones. The guy intrigues me. I would love to have the opportunity to have a purposeful conversation with him. It is no wonder that people thrive on his influence. They join his companies and buy seats on his airlines because of what they see being accomplished. They are drawn to his purpose, his vision, his life.

Through purposeful relationship, people will follow leaders and organizations from mission to mission, task to task, and glory to glory. They are drawn by purposeful influence because they see things being accomplished. They are swept up by the momentum, consumed in the vortex, pulled along by the vacuum created as the great movement gathers speed.

Like businesses, many Christian gatherings and groups thrive at the level of purposeful relationship; they grow spectacularly and successfully. And while there is nothing wrong with the transformative power of purposeful relationships—certainly they are better than positional or preferred relationships—there must be something more; a necessary and greater form of relationship.

It is normal to accept leaders and organizations for what they are accomplishing, but we must handle these associations with wisdom. For example, I know many people want to be ordained by the famous preacher, T.D. Jakes, because they see his success. And while it could be right for one person to be ordained by him, it could be wrong for another. Likewise, it could be right for one person to be ordained by Dutch Sheets and wrong for another person to seek it.

The key is that ordination must go beyond the influence of purposeful relationship. We must look beyond what the leader is accomplishing and determine if the ministry—the source level of gifting, anointing, and personality—is right for our emerging ministry. When we align ourselves with another, we must do so on a deeper level than merely wanting to be part of what we see them doing.

In business, I admire what Richard Branson is accomplishing. In reality, I would no more bond with him than I would attempt to play middle linebacker for the Tennessee Titans. It would not be a good fit relationally. (And I might need my spine realigned afterwards.) This is because I am different than Richard Branson. At our core, we are aligned along different vectors. My gifting is directed towards the Body of Christ; his is towards the marketplace. I owe and acknowledge my salvation to Jesus Christ; I am not sure where Richard's spiritual allegiance lies, but if it is centered on God, I've yet to hear of it. We are too divergent to be aligned, yet I admire him from afar just as I might admire a popular singer. I can't tell you if the late Waylon Jennings ever came to the cross, but he sang a mean song. His music often propelled me down the road when I needed a lift. Still, I never saw myself ever becoming his backup singer. I have my own God-given vision to pursue and accomplish, in Jesus' name.

Failing to understand the limits of purposeful influence, people get hurt when they can't seem to gain traction under one ministry or leader. The results they expected—the acknowledgment, the support, the validation and the promotion—don't always materialize. Yet they are strongly attracted to the minister and his or her work. They sense the momentum, they love the impact the ministry is having on the community and the church, and they want to be a part of it. This works for a while. But to grow under the tutelage of a ministry requires a level of intimacy that goes beyond the influence of purposeful relationship.

Under purposeful influence, leaders will be accepted and liked for what they are accomplishing and not the level of gifting and authority to the body of Christ.

Purposeful Idealism

When caught up in the momentum of a purposeful relationship, idealism can easily creep in. People enthralled with a ministry or other organization tend to overlook the problems. When we are focused on the accomplishments, the issues beneath the surface can seem a bit blurry.

That kind of blindness has a way of recoiling on a person, when suddenly the rose-colored glasses clear and everywhere he looks, there seem to be vast problems, personal failings, misdirection and masquerades. This can happen as the momentum in the organization slows, or when the person gets offended over something, growing angry or disillusioned. In truth, nothing is ever as good as it seems or as bad as it seems. As brilliant as a minister, a ministry, a business, an artist or entrepreneur seems to be in the beginning, they are no more worthy of the shameless accolades laid on them by idealistic devotees than they are deserving of the slights and accusations hurled as the scales fall from freshly focused eyes.

Both *illusion* and *disillusion* are rooted in deception. We tend to see what we want to see while looking for validation of our feelings. When swept up in the positive stream flowing from a great work, we identify with the grandeur, the sunny future, the endless possibilities that our optimism feeds us. But when the superstructure of our heart's ambitions begins to crumble, we need a reason for our crestfallen feelings, so we look for the faults, the failings, the shortcomings of the same organization that had elevated us in the first place. The sad result is that we begin to disengage and search for another, more "worthy" endeavor into which we can pour our energy.

At our church, we realize that the solution to this destructive cycle is balance. To achieve it, we follow one simple principle. We won't entertain complaints about anything in the church that the complainer is not willing to help change. We want people who are seeing problems to become part of the solution. For example, if a parent thinks the youth group needs help, we will listen, but in the end, she just might be offered a youth leader position. If a teenager thinks the worship music is too soft, he just might find himself apprenticed to the soundperson. When elderly people tell me that the roof leaks, I hand them a tool belt and point to the ladder. (No, even I won't do that. But it is a great system. I either get lots of volunteers or very few complainers. I must be doing something right!)

While the application can be a bit tricky, the principle behind this method is sound. I am always amazed at people who can identify everything wrong with a ministry—exactly how *God showed it to them*—but they have no clue how to fix it. So they don't try. Funny how God's personal revelation to them is devoid of anything positive. It's almost like God goes around finding fault with everything just like these people do. Well...maybe not so funny.

There is nothing wrong with identifying faults as long as the initiative to change is present as well. In our church, we have people who have been praying for years for improvement in certain areas. I know these people; I know their hearts; I see their commitment in action. Of course, I'm not claiming that our church, or any church, is perfect. Far from it. But I am trying to identify a process through which we move towards perfection. Complaining alone will not get us there. Idealism comes before fault-finding.

The fruit produced through a purposeful relationship will outshine the problems that develop, as long as we are open to receiving balance. A positive, life-based spirit will enable that balance. Every church has problems. Every company has problems. Where there are people, there are problems. Welcome to the human race; hope you brought your shovel. We all go through tests and trials. But when we get focused on the negatives, we lose the positive progression.

I recently bought a new laptop—one with an impeccable reputation for quality from a leading company. Guess what? It crashed three times! I mean—crashed hard. Each time, it took a long trip to the repair center and time spent to get the beast going again. Finally, on the third crash, the company stepped up and gave me a brand new unit—a better model than the one I had bought. Since then, I have had wonderful use of the machine...by far the best I've ever owned. But it came through a purposeful relationship with the company. I did not give up on them. I did not tie the ailing laptop to a chain and declare it the most expensive boat anchor ever. I did not call the newspapers and set it on fire in the middle of town. No, I kept working with the company, and they kept working with me. Today, I am blessed.

Chapter 11

Relational Covenants

A relationship is something we are.

All That Matters

Everything in life is a journey towards relational covenants. During his final hours on earth, Jesus told his disciples that they were no longer servants, but friends. In the next breath, he gave them the true nature of friendship:

> *Greater love has no one than this, than to lay down one's life for his friends.*

John 15:13

When Jesus referred to laying down one's life, he did not just mean dying. Indeed, Jesus did much more than die for humanity. In laying down his life, he set aside everything in his life with the Father for the chance to build life-giving relationship with us. He gave up everything for a time, and we must go and do likewise. Not that we abandon our lives, but we prioritize our lives, holding relationship above all else.

I have known extremely successful people who obtained all they ever dreamed of. Yet, even these who were blessed materially above all the earth came to one stark realization, that despite all they achieved and possessed, the only thing that matters in life is relationships. These are the true riches.

Relational covenants are the deepest of all relationships. They go beyond preference or alliance. They represent a heart bond that transcends all opposing forces. They function until God speaks otherwise.

Purpose and Conviction

To summarize what we have learned so far, in the Cave of Adullam—the place of deliverance—we relate to one another positionally as Pastor, Apostle, Captain or Madam Secretary. As we grow, we move into preferred relationships, living our lives based on our preferences. *I prefer to be at church tonight, or I prefer to go to the movies.* There are many choices available to a free people, and with these choices come the natural consequences. Inherent in our relational choices is the authority that we are willing to let influence us. Remember that we only accept the influence of authority to the degree that we are in relationship with the source of that authority. I will accept the authority of those closest to me much more readily and to a deeper extent than I will the authority of those of a superficial acquaintance.

As we arrive in Hebron—the place of development—we see a place where people begin to move out together, developing unity and effectiveness. We have traveled from preferred influence to purposeful influence, and we begin to focus on what an organization or ministry is actually doing. We begin to sense a divergence from our shallower ways of relating to authority, hearing a deeper call and realizing that answering that call requires something more than our preference. We have arrived at conviction.

Conviction is the quality that God cultivates in mature believers—those who can carry the greater responsibility. When we operate in conviction, we are far less likely to quit, turn back, or fail at our intended purpose. Conviction means God can *TRUST* us; we have become trustworthy.

Still, while conviction can hold us in place, it cannot give us a reason for being there. For that, we need something more. Purposeful relationships drive us to be where our heart is leading. Purposeful relationships, therefore, are the first dynamic of relational covenants.

David and Jonathan

When David and Jonathan met, David had just killed Goliath and his fame was spreading. What transpired afterwards illustrates the true nature of a relational covenant.

> *Now when he had finished speaking to Saul, the soul of Jonathan was knit to the soul of David, and Jonathan loved him as his own soul. Saul took him that day, and would not let him go home to his father's house anymore. Then Jonathan and David made a covenant, because he loved him as his own soul. And Jonathan took off the robe that was on him and gave it to David, with his armor, even to his sword and his bow and his belt.*

> 1 Samuel 18:1-4

While the rest of Israel was rejoicing over David's exploits—heralding him from afar—Jonathan saw deeper into the young conqueror's soul and bonded with him. Later, as tensions grew between the increasingly popular David and the rogue King Saul, it was Jonathan who provided the crucial support for David, even as both their lives hung in the balance.

And Jonathan said to David..."And you shall not only show me the kindness of the Lord while I still live, that I may not die; but you shall not cut off your kindness from my house forever, no, not when the Lord has cut off every one of the enemies of David from the face of the earth." So Jonathan made a covenant with the house of David, saying, "Let the Lord require it at the hand of David's enemies."

1 Samuel 20:11, 14-16

Finally, while fighting alongside his corrupt father, Jonathan fell at the sword of the Philistines. David grieved from the pit of his being, aching for his friend. Years later, now a king and having triumphed over all obstacles to achieving his destiny, David still acted on the relational covenant he had formed with Jonathan when he asked:

"Is there still anyone who is left of the house of Saul, that I may show him kindness for Jonathan's sake?"

2 Samuel 9:1

Indeed, there was—Jonathan's handicapped son Mephibosheth. Now, to put David's question in context, it must be understood that kindness to a preceding king's family was not customary, especially when that king had fought to kill his eventual successor. However, David was a man after God's heart; it was to God that David trusted and owed allegiance. There was no room for mindless vengeance in his ascension to the throne. But Mephibosheth did not realize this when David came calling. In fact, he was a bit scared.

Now when Mephibosheth the son of Jonathan, the son of Saul, had come to David, he fell on his face and prostrated himself. Then David said, "Mephibosheth?"

And he answered, "Here is your servant!"

So David said to him, "Do not fear, for I will surely show you kindness for Jonathan your father's sake, and will restore to you all the land of Saul your grandfather; and you shall eat bread at my table continually."

Then he bowed himself, and said, "What is your servant, that you should look upon such a dead dog as I?"

And the king called to Ziba, Saul's servant, and said to him, "I have given to your master's son all that belonged to Saul and to all his house. You therefore, and your sons and your servants, shall work the land for him, and you shall bring in the harvest, that your master's son may have food to eat. But Mephibosheth your master's son shall eat bread at my table always."...

Then Ziba said to the king, "According to all that my lord the king has commanded his servant, so will your servant do."

"As for Mephibosheth," said the king, "he shall eat at my table like one of the king's sons." ... So Mephibosheth dwelt in Jerusalem, for he ate continually at the king's table. And he was lame in both his feet.

2 Samuel 9:6-13

Here was relational covenant in action, reaching across generational lines which had been polluted with blood and were primed for vengeance. David's relationship with his fallen friend Jonathan overcame all and extended a blessing to a man that David never knew.

Relational Covenant

As we connect to leadership through a shared sense of purpose, we move out of the alliance born of positional or preferential relationship, and into a place where relational covenants are being established.

To put this in context, here is how David could have seen his relationship with Jonathan under varying relationships:

- Positional: *Cool, I'm getting to hang out with the king's son.*

- Preferred: *That Jonathan guy is fun. Wonder what he's doing tonight?*

- Purposeful: *Whoa! Jonathan is really trying to change things. I gotta join him!*

- Relational Covenant: *I love that man with all my heart. Nothing shall ever separate us.*

While alliances only work together until the task is accomplished or the need is met, relational covenants build a permanent relationship that functions until death do us part. Ephesians 4 tells us:

> *that we should no longer be children, tossed to and fro and carried about with every wind of doctrine, by the trickery of men, in the cunning craftiness of deceitful plotting, but, speaking the truth in love, may grow up in all things into Him who is the head—*

Christ—from whom the whole body, joined and knit together by what every joint supplies, according to the effective working by which every part does its share, causes growth of the body for the edifying of itself in love.

Ephesians 4:14-16

Through relational covenant, organizations are joined together by each member—each joint supplying their gift of authority and anointing to the team. Yet to be fully assembled, the leaders' hearts must be joined with the people as well as with other leaders. An organization can have the best leaders in the world, but without good people, those leaders are worthless. We need what every person can supply, and we need to be joined to them.

We can have prophetic revelation and the clearest vision of what God wants to do in an area, but it is going to take the gifts and talents of all to accomplish it. I think of it like a jigsaw puzzle. I'm not very good at puzzles; they require something called *patience*. But people who are good at puzzles tell me that they look for the smooth edges first. Put those together and you have a border—a boundary from which to build. I typically see God do the same thing in gathering a body of people. He appoints the smooth edges first— those who are of a pioneering spirit: apostles, prophets, and prayer warriors. It wouldn't make sense to start with teachers, for example, because there would be no one to teach. But soon there will be, and teachers will arrive, filling the center of the border with more and more talented people.

Where there is no revelation, the people cast off restraint; but happy is he who keeps the law.

Proverbs 29:18

As a ministry grows, apostolic vision and prophetic restraint (or guidance) comprises the smooth pieces that keep things in order. Congregations that are most successful find ways to integrate new people within this border almost immediately. When they can do that, they won't lose them. Puzzle pieces like to connect with other puzzle pieces; they need to be joined to feel whole. Those who become an integral part of the organization desire and receive accountably through alignment with the leadership team. They will be followers who seek a covenant that comes out of relationship, rather than a relationship that comes out of covenant. The former is desire-based; the latter is obligation-based. Let me explain.

What Is In a Name?

As we journey to understand relational covenants and how they are established, I want to explain why I have chosen the term *relational covenant.*

Back in the 70's and early 80's, there was a movement in the United States started by some great leaders of God. Referred to as the Discipleship Movement (or Shepherding Movement), it was about covenant relationships, seeking to engender accountability and character development. Unfortunately, it quickly devolved into legality. It essentially taught that if you had covenant relationship with someone, you were not able to make any decision without them being involved. Now, this worked alright when the decisions were the big-picture kind: should I change jobs, should I buy this house, should I move my family across the country? But little by little, the decision-making authority descended deeper into personal lives until the most intimate issues in an individual's life were laid bare on the altar of communal judgment.

To handle this superstructure of micro-management, pyramids of authority were formed from central locations as people began taking their orders from their shepherds rather than hearing from God. As you can imagine, this approach did not take long to decay into full-on bondage. For a while, I sat under a minister who followed this teaching, and I had to have his permission to borrow money for a car, change my address, or get a new phone line in the house. (Houses had phone lines back then; the phones were connected to wires.) Even though it began well-intentioned and was based on the concept of developing people through relationship, its controlling nature hurt more people than it helped.

Then one day, I was talking to the Lord about this and he said, *"I never want you to use the term 'covenant relationship' again."* At that time, I had enough relationship with God to pluck up my courage and ask the Almighty, *"Why? What's wrong with using that term?"*

In response, God showed me that when we use the phrase *covenant relationship*, the emphasis is on *covenant*—a binding agreement between two or more individuals. The problem with this emphasis is that, in our human nature, we tend to organize ourselves into hierarchies of leadership and management, focusing on the covenant aspect instead of the relationship aspect. This is because in the short-term, it is much easier to control people through covenant. They essentially have to do what they are told to do, period! In contrast, God told me that relationships are spiritual. As such, focusing on the covenant rather than the relationship kills the spiritual aspect of our existence.

Where a covenant is legal, relationships are spiritual. Relationship connects us in ways that we cannot see with natural eyes, nor understand with natural reasoning.

Paul told us of God:

> *Who also made us sufficient as ministers of the new covenant, not of the letter but of the Spirit; for the letter kills, but the Spirit gives life.*

2 Corinthians 3:6

Covenants, on the other hand, are based on law. They are greater than a contract but they have an element of a contract in the form of a binding agreement.

As my understanding of covenants and relationships grew, I asked the Lord if I could use the term *relational convenant* and teach it with a life emphasis. In answer, he spoke the term *relational covenant* to me as confirmation, and I've been teaching it that way ever since.

Through alignment with relational authority, followers will desire covenants that come out of relationship rather than relationship that comes out of covenant.

A covenant is something we do. A relationship is something we are.

What has kept Susan and me married for 40 years is not that we still have our marriage license from the Jurassic age. It's not like we take that worn sheepskin out of the desk, unroll it and say *Man! We have to stay married 'cause the ink hasn't faded yet.* No, it wasn't even the vows that we spoke 40 years ago. Instead, what keeps us together is the fact that we built a relationship on love and commitment. Naturally, our relationship is not perfect. But it is the loving relationship that keeps us together. Not the contract; not the marriage license; not the words that we spoke on that day that it rained rice and tin cans chased us down the street. No, it is not the covenant. It is the relationship. It is the love. It is who we are.

Today I can testify to the living power of relational covenants. I know people with whom I have ministered for twenty years, and while I first knew them as their function or title, we eventually grew into relational covenant. I began to see a more powerful, effective and meaningful bond than any legal binding. When one of us had a problem, we knew we could call on the other. We became friends who have stood with each other as our children have gone through hard times, our ministries have ebbed and flowed, and our businesses have launched on fledging wings. As we grew together, all pretense and formality was dropped. We could be ourselves. We have prayed together, wept together, and shared God's harvest together. I can tell you from first-hand experience that the heart-to-heart bond of a relational covenant is what Jesus desires for all of us.

Relational Covenant Influence

When we are in relational covenant with people, our effectiveness in influencing their lives is greatly enhanced. Through the spirit, I can influence someone from across a room or halfway across the globe. Through relational covenant, I can sense things about those who are nearest my heart. I can do all these things and more because relationships are spiritual.

I have a friend in England; his time is seven hours ahead of mine in Mississippi. The other day we were talking by phone and he said, *"Clay, you've been praying for me, haven't you?"* And I said, *"Yes, indeed!"* In fact, I had been praying a lot for him; I had a burden and went to prayer for days. This shows me that through the spirit, his life was affected by my spirit even though he was thousands of miles away in a land where people drink warm beer and talk funny.

Of course, I am not talking about witchcraft, which inhabits people's lives for evil purposes. I am talking about praying blessings over people according to Holy Spirit, reaching folks across the seas of the spirit where time and space are different than in the physical realm. Relationships are spiritual; as such, they follow the laws of the spirit. Because human beings are spiritual, these things can occur anywhere. All it takes is a relational covenant to touch someone close to you through an authentic bond.

Twins often experience this bonding from the womb. I recall a story of twins who lived apart and never knew each other. They had been separated at birth and neither one ever knew of the other. One day, one of them started having abdominal pain while the other was having an appendicitis attack. The twin with the sympathetic pain actually wrote in her journal, *I believe I have a twin out there having an appendicitis.* Years later, they finally met and compared notes. To their mutual amazement, their lives paralleled one another's to great detail.

Relationship Changes Everything

The first time I saw Susan she was about 9 years old. She had been out in the sun all summer and her hair was a lighter color then. She was over on the school athletic field doing a broad jump. She had a ponytail, cowboy boots and blue jeans, and I thought *WOW!* Through our school years, we became good friends. We never dated; we just enjoyed each other's company. We rode bicycles together; we rode horses together; we rode motorcycles together; we did all of that. We went frog gigging. We did all these things together and never dated until she was in college. Yet there was always a righteous attraction. I thought she was the prettiest thing on earth. I proposed to her 14 times. But I was a heathen back then. Sometimes the force that caused me to propose came out of a bottle.

The day she finally accepted my proposal, I saw something different in her. She had driven home from college and was getting out of her car. She wasn't even supposed to be coming home that weekend. When I hugged her, she looked me in the eye, and I thought

Yep, its gonna happen this time. I knew then that we were on our way to building a relational covenant, and it changed everything.

More Than Unity

Relational covenant leads us to deployment. We are ready to move out. We want to go to work, fulfill our calling, and return jubilant over our accomplishments. Through relational covenant, we become connected with a purpose, gain a greater understanding of our place in that momentum, and find ourselves growing in unity with a group of people. But there is something greater than simply being unified.

Let's think for a moment about what happens to a group of people when the emphasis is solely on unity. Soon, everybody starts to look alike, talk alike, think alike and act alike. What's worse—those who resist this process and stand out as individuals are branded as rebels, un-teachable, a corrupting influence. They are eventually ostracized, kicked out of the group and made an example to the rest. It quickly becomes apparent to the casual observer that this group's goal is not unity at all; it is conformity. And conformity, my friend, is *deformity*.

In my ministry, I expect diversity. I don't want everybody sounding like me, dressing like me, or (*Lord help us!*) looking like me. I have a friend who had lunch with five members of a local cult. To a man, they each had the same clothing, same beard, same haircut, and what was most surprising: they even had the same smell. These people were in deep bondage to each other, and they were losing their souls in the process. See, I can't start to look like you unless I give up a part of me—the *me* that God created me to be. There is only one Clay Nash. Praise God! But even better, there is only one of you. And you. And you. And even *you*. God made each and every one of us unique, just like everyone else! (OK—don't think too hard on that one.)

Diversity brings strength. Through our commitment to one another, we form relational covenants and the desire to be trained and matured into a greater level of Christ-likeness. However, to be like Christ does not mean to be one way. Jesus will look differently through each of us. Just as white light is comprised of all the visible colors, so each of us will reveal some portion of the spectrum that is found in God. He is too big to be contained in one person, or a dozen persons, or a trillion persons. When we taste the diversity of mankind, we sense the vastness of our Lord and Creator in every culture, generation, and individual. Because we are different, we grow stronger.

Catching the Anointing

One of the strengths arising from relational covenants is the sharing of anointing—God's spiritual power to accomplish his will. To effectively catch an anointing, you need to form close associations with those who are carrying the anointing, and you must humble yourself.

Years ago, the Lord told me to go to Orlando where Benny Hinn still had his church. I did not know Benny Hinn personally; I only knew of him. But I had a great relationship with his youth pastor, Carlos. I had actually spoken to his youth group, and Carlos began bringing the youth up from Orlando Christian Center to our congregation every spring during Spring Break.

God's word to me was very specific: *I want you to go down and go to this service. I am going to impart something to you that you need.* Being a practical man and knowing the crowds that flocked to Benny's meetings in those days, I called Pastor Carlos, said I was coming and could he get me a good seat, because I really wanted to catch whatever God had for me. To my mind, Benny was going to lay hands on me, speak to me personally, and probably prophesy over me, speaking deep truths that my soul needed to hear.

You'd think I would have known better—putting God in a box like that. But I didn't.

That weekend, Susan and I drove to Orlando and decided to make it a dual purpose trip: part vacation and part receiving from Benny Hinn. We took the kids to Disney World and planned to attend Benny's meeting on Sunday night. Carlos had told me earlier that he got us seats on the second row from the stage, right on the end. Now, in terms of Christian meetings, that was the equivalent of 50 yard-line seats at the Superbowl. I was excited. We were going to see Benny Hinn live. He was going to call me up, pray for me; we were going to connect; God was going to move; our spirits would flow together.... Oh, how I can dream!

Well, we got to the meeting that night but never connected with Carlos. We waited and waited while droves of people poured in and grabbed the first available seats. Finally, we heard that Carlos and his family were in a minor car wreck. They are OK, but they would miss the meeting, the consequence being that we never got our chosen seats up front. To make matters worse, because we did not get a seat when crowds started arriving, we are shuttled to the nosebleed section, stuck way up in the balcony.

Now, like I said, I am a bit of a dreamer. And like all dreamers, I can become disillusioned when my image of what is to take place clashes with God's image. (Guess who wins?)

So I found myself in Orlando in obedience to God, freshly sunburned from a day in Mickey Mouse land, stuck way up in the balcony where nobody knows I'm there but the pigeons and the angels, and I have this attitude. *God you told me to come down here, and I am up here and Benny Hinn ain't gonna know I am up here and I am not gonna get hands laid on me and I am not gonna get what you want me to have.* Yeah, I had it bad. And the Lord spoke to me and said, *"If you don't change your attitude, not only are you not going to get anything, you're going to leave here with less than you came with."*

Well, that got my attention. I took off my mouse ears, got on my knees and began to repent. It was theater type seating, making it difficult to kneel between those folding seats with all the gum and goo on the floor, but I managed, humbling myself before God, the birds, and a few snickering angels.

That night, Benny preached for hours and nothing much happened. But I didn't care anymore. I was right with God; that's all that mattered. Then towards the end of the service Benny walked down an aisle, waved his hand at a lower section of the crowd, and everybody in those seats fell to the floor under the power of Holy Spirit. I moved to the edge of my seat. Then he walked farther into the crowd and stood right below where I was sitting in the balcony. He tilted his head up and hollered for everybody in our area of the balcony to stand up. Ripe with expectancy, we all jumped to our feet. Next, he said to join hands, so we did. Finally, smiling, he bellowed, *"You came all the way to Orlando to get it, didn't you? Well here it is!"* And he slung his hand towards us. When he did that, whole rows of us fell backwards. Everybody was staggered. For my part, the anointing hit me so hard that I flew into the seats behind me with the wind knocked out of me. I lay motionless for several minutes, dreaming beyond reason, basking in the wonderful realities that comprised God's *NOW!*

So what was *it*? What did Benny Hinn dispense that night? The Bible calls it the anointing. But what is that? Simply put: we know a tree by its fruit. After that night, I returned to my ministry and began to see an increase in signs, wonders and miracles. People and situations that previously remained beyond the reach of my spiritual ability were now being touched by the power of God in a fresh and dynamic way. I call that the anointing; I call that good. God is good.

He who walks with wise men will be wise, but the companion of fools will be destroyed.

Proverbs 13:20

Chapter 12

Principles of Relational Covenants

'Till death do us part.

In walking through relational covenants, I've learned five principles over the years, gleaning from the teaching of many Christian leaders, Ron Corzine among them. Here is a distillation of their teaching as it pertains to relational covenants.

#1 The Relationship Principle.

We should treasure the God-given relationships in our lives above any problem which would try to destroy them. Before God, the relationship outweighs the issues. As Christians, we don't have to be right; we just have to be reconciled. When the relationship principle is in proper order, we first address the health of our relationship before attempting to deal with the issues in the relationship.

I have been married for over 40 years and there are times when I say to Susan, "*I am sorry I messed it up, I did it wrong,*" only for her to discover later that what really caused the contention came from her side, not mine. But I was willing to neutralize the toxin in our relationship by saying *sorry* as long as it made us reconciled, working together and talking again. If we can keep communicating, we can overcome anything.

Susan and I were both born again in the early years of our marriage. Not only were we newlyweds, we were also new Christians, completely untrained and unfamiliar with the ways of God. We did a lot of prayer in those days—often praying in separate places of the house we called our prayer closets, and while our hearts were honest before God, I can't say that our prayers were spot-on with the will of God. It seemed that the thing we prayed about most of the time was each other—go figure.

I recall being in my prayer closet saying: *God! I can't live with Susan like she is; you've got to change her.* Now, in those days my dad had a million dollar policy on me. Which is probably why Susan spent a lot of time in her prayer closet saying: *God, you need to kill Clay; he has a lot of insurance.* Oh, thank God for unanswered prayer.

Then one day, a particularly divisive issue came up between us and I went to my prayer closet, intending to tell God again that he needed to change Susan, but instead, this is what came out: *Lord, if Susan never changes, will you change me so I can live with her like she is?*

On that the very same day, Susan was praying: *Lord, you don't have to kill him, just change me so I can live with him.*

That was the beginning of our marriage. We both realized that trying to change the other—even through the forced hand of the Almighty—was not working. In fact, it was a negative form of manipulation that could easily lead to greater evil. From that day forward, we both allowed God to work on us, changing the things that we needed to change so that we could love the other more selflessly. And for my part, I learned never to cross that woman… ever!

Just as in marriage, healthy relationships are also vital to a congregation. Those in leadership should seek to be in relational covenant with every person in their care. Because of this, it is important for leaders to sit with those they lead and assess the health of the relationship together. In our congregation, it is common for me to ask probing questions (because no one likes to come out and be negative). I sometimes ask, *"Have I done anything to disappoint you? Is there anything in the way that I handle things that you would like me to change? Are there any promises I have made that I have forgotten and not kept?"* These issues are important to my heart. I realize that unless the relationships are healthy, the fruit from them will not be healthy.

On the other side of leadership, every person in a congregation needs to understand from God exactly where they need to be, and they need to be committed to being there. Nothing bothers me more than to hear people say *"God brought me here and I will remain until he takes me somewhere else."* I realize that this sounds noble, but let's look at the statement closer. I have seen too many people led away from their true place of service through offense, wandering, or misplaced ambition. What we think leaves the door open for God to move us on, is really allowing the enemy to go to work on us until we get frustrated enough to transfer somewhere else.

#2 The Time Principle.

We should not judge the relationship by the quantity of time we spend together, but the quality of time we spend together. Fifteen minutes of good quality time outweighs three hours of mindless pursuits—even if we are watching TV! We should choose to value the fellowship based on God's purpose for the time together. While we are meeting, what are we talking about? What is the purpose?

What are we building together? Are we actively engaged, or would we be better off alone? Quality time means we are together for a purpose, intentionally building the relationship and all that emerges from it.

#3 The Lazarus Principle.

Lazarus was the man who Jesus raised after being dead for four days. The Jews told Jesus not to bother praying, for he stank on the fourth day.

The Lazarus principle is simply this: we should not take more than four days to process any offence, confusion, or unresolved issue that threatens our relationship. To do otherwise allows the stench and decay of death to pollute our relationship. We cannot build relational covenants without effectively processing our wounds and releasing our grudges.

I constantly remind my people that if something I do (or don't do) causes a problem, to please not let it linger. Do not wait, but come to me and let's get it resolved. It could just be a distorted perception or a misunderstanding. Whatever the case, let's address it before decay sets in and it starts to stink. Just as the Jews were inferring when they pointed to the expiration date on the grave, it is a whole lot easier to raise a body from the grave if it has not had time to decay.

Memory is our friend if we can act on these things quickly. When someone comes to me and says, *"A year ago when I started coming to your church, you said this and it really offended me,"* all I can do is ask forgiveness. I might not even have said it, but I can't remember everything that was said a year ago. Some days, I can't remember what I said yesterday! But I've learned that asking forgiveness is my ticket out of offenses. Let's apologize and move on. If I really did something wrong, I'll probably do it again, and then we'll deal with it promptly so we can both learn and grow beyond it.

Don't let things fester. Most people avoid confrontation. Yet, healthy relationships are built through healthy communication, and that includes confrontation. *I don't like the shirt you have on or the boots you preach in.* Come and tell me that! I might not pay any attention to it, but it might make you feel better. Seriously, some of the toughest confrontations I've had later served to bring me closer to the confronter.

Don't let problems build until the relationship becomes diseased. When my dad finally got the diagnosis that he had colon cancer, he had been bleeding for a couple of years. It breaks my heart. If he would have not been so hard-headed, and been willing to see the doctor when it first started, a simple operation could have put him back on his feet—certainly as hard-headed as ever but at least cancer-free!

Just as it is necessary to confess our faults and ask forgiveness, it is also important to know how to receive an apology. It must be done in love; this is not the time to vent your malice at the offender, no matter how justly deserved. An apology is a humbling time. Accept it in grace, and that will empower the person to change.

Before I was born-again, I was an adulterer. When I got saved, I confessed it to Susan, and to her credit, she never once brought it up or threw it in my face. I appreciate that. I had a lot to repent of when I got saved, and she has forgiven me and let it go. In turn, I have striven every day of my life to be worthy of her love, faithfulness, and trust. That is Kingdom; that is relational covenant.

We need to grasp the true spiritual nature of forgiveness. We are not going to stand before the judgment seat of Christ one day and hear God say, *"You asked me to forgive you for lying before you were born again, but I really want to talk to you about it now."* No, he cast our sins into the Sea of Forgetfulness, never to think about them again. We need to do the same.

> *He will again have compassion on us, and will subdue our iniquities. You will cast all our sins into the depths of the sea.*

> Micah 7:19

#4 The Integrity Principle.

The Integrity Principle tells us to be extremely careful how we share our relationship problems with anyone else, especially our spouses. Why? Because it can burden them unnecessarily. I don't go home and tell Susan everything—certainly not the immediate issues. Let me give an example.

Let's say that after reading this book, someone comes up to me and says, *"I just want you to know that this was the poorest teaching I have ever read in my life. It was awful, it ruined my life, and now everybody hates me because they think I'm paranoid!"*

Of course, that's not pleasant to hear. But if he catches me on a good day, I will likely be gracious and reply, *"I'm sorry you feel that way. I don't agree with you about the book, but I will pray about it and see what the Lord says."*

Now, if I were to go home that evening and tell Susan what was said and who said it, she could become agitated. *Is this person attacking my husband? What does he know about writing a book? How dare he unload on Clay like that?* Notice she is out of the loop in the communication between me and this person, but she is unfortunately bearing the fruit of the man's issue. She now has a second-hand offense. She is offended on my behalf and is only getting my side of the story, fueling her well-meaning but one-sided defense of me and raising her hackles.

Later, during the night, let's say that the Lord wakes that offended man, and he enters into prayer before God. Before he goes to work, he calls me and apologizes. *"Hey, I'm really sorry. It's not your fault. Turns out I'm not really paranoid; everybody IS out to get me."*

The important thing is that he realizes his offense. He really didn't like the book (which is fine), but he understands that the book did not wreck his life and neither did I. Praise God!

I'm fine with all of this, but Susan, who did not hear the man's apology, is still stewing—needlessly, in this case. But by deferring the communication of a minor offense, I could have saved her mountains of agitation and the need to repent of any ill-will towards this gentleman who obviously doesn't know a great literary work when he sees one.

Some things are best left to ourselves and God—especially the people-stuff.

#5 Communication In Relational Covenants.

When relational covenant exists, it is not always necessary to receive explicit directions for us to operate in harmony with the present authority. It is our hearts that speak and bear testimony to the bond undergirding the relationship. Jesus made that startlingly clear when he healed ten lepers and only one returned to give honor to his healer.

Now it happened as He went to Jerusalem that He passed through the midst of Samaria and Galilee. Then as He entered a certain village, there met Him ten men who were lepers, who stood afar off. And they lifted up their voices and said, "Jesus, Master, have mercy on us!"

So when He saw them, He said to them, "Go, show yourselves to the priests." And so it was that as they went, they were cleansed.

And one of them, when he saw that he was healed, returned, and with a loud voice glorified God, and fell down on his face at His feet, giving Him thanks. And he was a Samaritan.

So Jesus answered and said, "Were there not ten cleansed? But where are the nine? Were there not any found who returned to give glory to God except this foreigner?" And He said to him, "Arise, go your way. Your faith has made you well."

Luke 17:11-19

Notice the apparent contradiction between Jesus' words and his actions. The nine lepers who did not return were doing <u>exactly what Jesus had instructed them to do</u>. They were going to show themselves to the priests. Yet, it was only the tenth leper who, on an unscheduled detour, ran back to thank him. It was also he who received Jesus' praise. Obviously, Jesus was rewarding the leper's initiative over and above his blind obedience.

We can find a scriptural shadow of this with the great prophet Elijah and his student/servant Elisha. Elijah was obviously seeking to develop his student who pursued relational covenant with him. But as Elijah was nearing the end of his time on earth, it appeared that he just wanted to be alone. But isn't it interesting that when Elijah told his servant to remain behind, Elisha refused?

And it came to pass, when the Lord was about to take up Elijah into heaven by a whirlwind, that Elijah went with Elisha from Gilgal. Then Elijah said to Elisha, "Stay here, please, for the Lord has sent me on to Bethel." But Elisha said, "As the Lord lives, and as your soul lives, I will not leave you!" So they went down to Bethel.

2 Kings 2:1-2

Even saying *please* did not get the younger prophet to obey his master. So finally relenting, Elijah allowed Elisha to accompany him. Personally, I suspect that he had little choice. But the process continued as Elijah told Elisha a second time to stay put:

Elijah said to him, "Elisha, please stay here, for the Lord has sent me to Jericho." But he said, "As the Lord lives, and as you yourself live, I will not leave you." So they came to Jericho.

2 Kings 2:4

Finally, a third time, Elijah implored Elisha to remain behind.

Then Elijah said to him [Elisha], "Stay here, please, for the Lord has sent me on to the Jordan." But he said, "As the Lord lives, and as your soul lives, I will not leave you!" So the two of them went on.

2 Kings 2:6

OK, so either this kid has a death-wish in defying the mightiest prophet in the land—the guy who slaughtered the prophets of Baal—or he knew something was up. Either way, Elisha clearly was not going to leave Elijah's side. His soul was knit to Elijah through relational covenant as David and Jonathan's souls were united.

These guys were a unit and nothing was coming between them, not even the temporal wishes of an aging prophet going to meet his maker on the other side of the Jordan River.

Finally, we see the fruit of this bond. Just as Jesus blessed the tenth leper, Elisha received a great blessing for his apparent impertinence.

> *And so it was, when they had crossed over, that Elijah said to Elisha, "Ask! What may I do for you, before I am taken away from you?" Elisha said, "Please let a double portion of your spirit be upon me."*

> 2 Kings 2:9

Incredibly, Elisha did receive a double portion. Fantastic! No words of instruction were spoken to guide Elisha's actions, only the imperative of a bonded heart—a soul joined in love and service, receiving the greatest reward.

Finally, we can look to Ruth as the epitome of relational covenants. Counted in the genealogy of Jesus even though she was from Moab, it was her oath to her mother-in-law that earned her that blessing. Despite Naomi's wishes that Ruth leave her and return to her homeland, Ruth declared her unwavering allegiance to remain with Naomi throughout hard times and an uncertain future:

> *But Naomi said, "Turn back, my daughters; why will you go with me? Are there still sons in my womb, that they may be your husbands? Turn back, my daughters, go—for I am too old to have a husband. If I should say I have hope, if I should have a husband tonight and should also bear sons, would you wait for them till they were grown? Would you restrain yourselves from having husbands? No, my daughters;*

for it grieves me very much for your sakes that the hand of the Lord has gone out against me!"

Then they lifted up their voices and wept again; and Orpah kissed her mother-in-law, but Ruth clung to her.

And she said, "Look, your sister-in-law has gone back to her people and to her gods; return after your sister-in-law." But Ruth said:

"Entreat me not to leave you,
Or to turn back from following after you;
For wherever you go, I will go;
And wherever you lodge, I will lodge;
Your people shall be my people,
And your God, my God.
Where you die, I will die,
And there will I be buried.
The Lord do so to me, and more also,
If anything but death parts you and me."

Ruth 1:11-17

Who can define relational covenant any better than Ruth? I can't. So let's leave our discussion here.

Chapter 13

Final Thoughts

Our deep heart's core...

When Jesus walked the earth, he was greeted by crowds who saw him as a teacher, a healer, a provider, and the Messiah who would rescue them from the oppression of Rome. While they accepted his bread, entertained his parables, and dreamed of his deliverance, few could accept his authority regarding God's truth. Others only saw Joseph's son, and so they rejected him.

Later, a smaller group gathered around Jesus—people who attended to his needs, sharing a passion for his ministry and clinging to his words. Seventy of this group were sent out in the authority of Jesus' anointing, and they returned rejoicing that even demons obeyed their authority. Eventually, however, many of these people became offended by his teaching and disillusioned with the direction of his ministry, so they rejected him.

Those who remained from this fallout were 12 disciples burning with conviction and desire. It was into these few that Jesus poured his deepest teaching and trust, leading them into an intimate understanding of the Father, imparting an authority that the crowds could never receive nor the 70 retain. Yet, even as Jesus developed these 12, there were disagreements, misunderstandings, blindness, denial, and eventually betrayal. Yet three grew closer to him, sharing his secrets and struggles, and one came closest to his heart—the disciple whom Jesus loved.

As Jesus hung on the cross, pouring out his life for all of mankind, forging a relational covenant with the Father that the world had never known, he spoke to his closest disciple and conveyed his last earthly treasure—the care of his mother.

When Jesus arose from the grave, he first met a women who had been close to him—not one of the crowds, or the group of 70, or even the 12 disciples. Instead, he greeted Mary and passed on to her words of relational covenant bought with his blood and sealed with his spirit: *I am ascending to my Father and your Father, and to my God and your God* (John 20:17). There could be no closer bond, no greater relationship, no deeper covenant or more profound peace. All had been fulfilled…at great price.

How we approach Jesus and his ministry today is up to us. We can gather with the crowds, calling out for him to feed us, rescue us, and protect us from our oppression. Or we can gather under his service for a time, casting off when it upsets us, retreating back to the anonymity of the amorphous gatherings to nurse our wounds. But if we honor our conviction to his work, we will gather under his authority and grow closer to the Father's heart. Relational and bonded, we will admit him into our deep heart's core—something we only thought we did when we hailed him from the crowds. Now, walking in the authentic authority that brings his life to ours, we will learn to share in the fellowship of his suffering and the power of his resurrection.

All authority is relational.

Further Information

If you would like further information on this or any other subject, feel free to contact me at: ClayRNash@gmail.com. I or my staff would be pleased to speak with you.